350/14

The Positive
Power of
Praising
People

"Is there power in praising people? Absolutely! The potential for touching the lives of those around you is unlimited when you utilize Jerry Twentier's principles of PraisePower!"

Anthony Robbins
Unlimited Power
and
Awaken the Giant Within

"The best management/human relations book I've read this year! Not just for managers, this book is perfect for anyone who makes contact with other human beings. Twentier's advice puts the power of positive feedback at the reader's fingertips."

Jimmy Calano, CEO
CareerTrack, **Boulder, Colorado**

"Jerry Twentier tells us with such clarity how to put to work the living power of praising people! Like the woman in the proverb, this book is more valuable than rubies!"

Dottie Walters
Speak and Grow Rich

"Love your book! It was Rockefeller who said 'I will pay more for the ability to deal with people than for any commodity under the sun.' Learning the power of praising people to success is the key to dealing with people. It WORKS!"

Mary Kay Ash, CEO
Mary Kay Cosmetics, Inc.

"Why hasn't this book been written before now? My best advice is read this gem of human relations! It's delightful! It's dynamic! It delivers!"

**Dear Abby
Abigail Van Buren**

"In the quest for healthier hearts, we cannot afford to discount either the power of the emotions or the potential of the healing word. If put into practice, *The Positive Power of Praising People* will improve our day-to-day relationships and maybe even our blood pressures. I am initiating my own praise campaign by applauding Jerry's book. His topic is unique, his style lighthearted, and his message unforgettable. In fact, I know of no one who would not benefit from following his advice."

**Denton A. Cooley, M.D.
Texas Heart Institute, Houston, Texas**

"Exceptionally well written! Exceptionally substantive! Exceptionally helpful! If God Himself enjoys and responds to praise, how could we be any different? Thanks Jerry, for underscoring this vital and practical principle!"

**Pat Boone, Entertainer
Los Angeles, California**

"Here is a book that is positive, uplifting, and most helpful. It shows us how to get along in this world and make the most of our opportunities. Every person who reads this book will be blessed by it! It will help us to become happier persons and make others happy."

Dr. Charles L. Allen

"A powerful, eye-opening realization to the basic needs of the people that are most important to us . . . the very people that make us what we are! As a father, a husband, and a United States Senator, I have become increasingly aware of the importance of praise to those around me. *The Positive Power of Praising People* provides the insight to a simple yet remarkable concept which can result in extraordinarily positive and powerful ramifications for everyone involved."

Mark O. Hatfield
United States Senator, Oregon

The Positive Power of Praising People

JERRY D. TWENTIER

THOMAS NELSON PUBLISHERS
Nashville

Published in Nashville, Tennessee, by Thomas Nelson, Inc.

Scripture quotations are from the NEW KING JAMES VERSION
of the Bible. Copyright © 1979, 1980, 1982, Thomas Nelson,
Inc., Publishers.

Library of Congress Cataloging-in-Publication Data

Twentier, Jerry.
    The positive power of praising people / Jerry Twentier.
      p. cm.
    ISBN 0-8407-6770-6 (hc)
    1. Praise. 2. Interpersonal relations. 3. Motivation
(Psychology) I. Title.
BF637.P7T94   1993
158'.2—dc20   93–31323
                                              CIP

Printed in the United States of America.
1 2 3 4 5 6 7 — 98 97 96 95 94 93

To Mom and Dad
for giving me faith and focus,
foundation and frame.
For is it not true the
frame makes even the
plainest of pictures
appear to be a
work of art?

To the happy memory
of Lucy Twentier
who, for a hundred
Septembers, graced us with
a portrait of poise and praise!

For the creation
of this book,
the best of my
thanks to you—
my mentors, my
heroes, my friends.

You have made
the difference!

How will you know
unless I tell you?

Dr. Charles L. Allen
Rick Alvarado
Chuck Arena
Mary Kay Ash
Rev. Earl Banning
Tom Bates
Pat Boone
Nathaniel Branden, Ph.D.
Jimmy Calano
Denton Cooley, M.D.
Deborah Dion
Corky Epperson
Barbara Glasgow
Dan Glasgow
Barbara Gurley
George Haley
Senator Mark Hatfield
Cesar Hernandez
Alex Horvath
Joyce Houlette
Dan Jenkins

Michael Lebovitz
Debbie McClanahan
Justin McClanahan
Linda McElwaney
Becky Maracich
Louise Mears
Grant Mitchell
Jim Morgan
Thomas O'Donnell
Jonathan Parker, Ph.D.
Patrick Richoux
Anthony Robbins
Jeneanne Sims
Abigail Van Buren
Joe Vitale
Bill Wallace
Dottie Walters
Mike Warren
Dr. Ben Williams
Jo Ann Williams
Dr. Mike Wronkovich

CONTENTS

PART THREE
Pursue a Higher Standard of Learning

PART FOUR
Pursue a Higher Standard of Loving

FOREWORD

From the Desk Of

DENTON A. COOLEY, M.D.

The topic of Jerry Twentier's book may seem somewhat remote from my own field of cardiovascular surgery. The idea of praise as "lifting up," however, recalls the ancient command to "lift up your *hearts*," as intoned in religious liturgies through the ages.

The value of praise has been recognized since biblical times. In the Psalms and many other sacred writings, praise tends to be associated with gratitude, thanksgiving, and celebration, all of which gladden the *heart*. Our English word *praise* is derived from the Latin noun *pretium*, which means *worth* or *price*. Things that are highly valued, or praiseworthy, are called *precious*, a term that is also derived from *pretium*.

From time immemorial, the heart has been viewed as the seat of man's emotions and even of his soul. In the quest for healthier hearts, we cannot afford to discount either the power of the emotions or the potential of the healing word.

During the past ten years, there has been increasing evidence that emotional states affect the immune system and that the mind and body influence each other in previously unsuspected ways. Some researchers even claim that emotions affect wound healing. Perhaps these insights will one day change the way we view physiology.

Meanwhile, there is no question that effective communication between the brain and the various organ systems is a primary requirement for harmonious bodily functioning. Surely, constructive communication between one human being and another is no less crucial for emotional well-being.

If put into practice, *The Positive Power of Praising People* will improve our day-to-day relationships and maybe even our blood pressures. Praise is the easiest and least expensive way to compensate one's employees, friends, and loved ones; to keep morale high; and to further interpersonal harmony.

I am initiating my own praise campaign by applauding Jerry's book. His topic is unique, his style lighthearted, and his message unforgettable. In fact, I know of no one who would not benefit from following his advice.

Denton A. Cooley, M.D.
Surgeon-in-Chief, Texas Heart Institute

PREFACE

Harsh winds of gray December whipped against my topcoat as I got out of the car. Sidestepping puddles, I trudged toward the mailbox.

Torrential winter rains dampened my already gloomy spirits. No umbrella could shield the downpour of emotions flooding inside me. The recent loss of a promising career, a financial crisis, and an impending divorce loomed like an unending thunderstorm on the horizon. Reaching into the mailbox, I drew out a small yellow envelope bearing unfamiliar handwriting. Tearing it open, I read welcome words from a friend:

Hi Jerry! Bet you're wondering why I'm writing, huh? Well, here goes: I miss you. I miss your laughter and your smile . . . and hey, how else will you know unless I tell you?

Instantly, it seemed like June! Rays of a summer day warmed me from the inside out. I felt energized all the way down to my soggy soles! Someone noticed! Precisely when I was feeling insignificant, a fellow human acknowledged my presence.

Rereading my treasured note again, something *new* captured my gaze. The final phrase intrigued me:

How else will you know unless I tell you?

Fact is, I wouldn't have known. None of us can know what emotional gems lie buried in the hearts and minds of others—until we see or hear some evidence.

In this fast-paced computerized era, most of us tend to squelch our true feelings. It's not "professional" to be emotional. That infrequent occasion when appreciation is most often voiced comes at the close of a career or even at the end of a life—unfortunately, too late to benefit the recipient.

After twenty-plus years in various environments of human relations, I am continually astounded by the magical, positive manner in which each of us responds to sincere appreciation and praise—and the tragic consequences that can occur when we neglect to voice our praise! Heartfelt applause and praise is rare, but nourishing. Within its contents are the elements of love, compassion, and amazing power! Even more amazing, there has never been a book dedicated solely to the principle of PraisePower—until now!

Wonderful as this concept is, I have to confess it is not an original. More than nineteen centuries ago, Christ led His dozen trusted associates aloft to a mountain retreat for final instructions before sending them out to spread His message. There, among other subjects, Christ underlined the foundation for all human relations—both personal and professional—in one brief sentence: "Therefore, whatever you want men to do to you, do also to them." The words were not for their ears only. The universal blueprint given that day continues to be amazingly relevant in our own quest for a higher standard of living!

While the ideas here are unique, I'm relieved to say the underlying principles are not original with me. If they were, they would still be unproven and lacking guarantees. The concepts of praise and human interaction in this book are not only practical, powerful, and phenomenally effective, but are in congruence with the heart of Scripture. And that, I'm confident in saying, IS guaranteed!

My compliments to you for considering the message of this book. May you discover your own personal, positive power in praising people! How else will they know unless you tell them?

It's not just a question. It's an *answer!*

ONE

Pursue a Higher Standard of Living

◆

We make a living by what we get.
We make a life by what we give.

◆

Chapter Objectives

O Realize our need for approval is as essential as air, food, and water!

O Make a living by what you get. Make a life by what you give.

O Invest in the happiness of others. Spend freely from the riches within you.

O Find the good and praise it!

O Put it in writing! Document your applause for lasting effect.

O Circulate all the good you hear about others.

O Employ the keys to successful praising to enjoy a key to successful living.

Sitting on the sofa in our tiny apartment one October day in 1983, my wife matter-of-factly mentioned that she had just phoned her dad in Ohio. Flying his private plane, he was en route to Houston to get her and she would not be coming back.

Bewildered, I began scrambling for a quick solution to change her mind. Wouldn't she reconsider the five years we had invested together? No. It was a closed subject.

The following day, three of us rode solemnly to a small airstrip in southeast Houston where the plane was poised for departure. Our somber mood matched the gray clouds overhead. Awkward attempts at small talk accented the final moments as the bags were loaded.

In one desperate final plea, I called her name and blurted out recklessly, "What happened to us?"

Staring at me through unclouded eyes void of emotion, she uttered a single phrase with indisputable certainty:

"Jerry, you don't need me."

With that, she turned, mounted the steps, and disappeared inside the tiny aircraft.

In shock, I watched the plane taxi down the airstrip. Rain began to fall lightly as the plane left the runway, angled sharply upward, and vanished into the cloud cover.

"We can see farther through a tear," explained Lord Byron, "than through a telescope." My insight became painfully clear as the haunting echo of her parting words gradually settled like the raindrops around me. "You don't need me?" I repeated incredulously. Of course I needed her!

Had I ever *told* her? Well, no, not exactly. But why didn't she *know* that?

How simple it all should have—could have—been! She taught me a costly lesson that day, and I'm sharing it with you. Sincere, heartfelt golden phrases of endearment can secure the complexion of your relationships: "I love you. I need you. You are important to me."

Why hadn't I told her?

Transplanted from the comfort zone of home and family, this young bride of twenty-two had sought a new identity with me. Busy with my own aspirations and interests, I neglected to let her know she was a vital part of my life. Engrossed in my own goals, I shut her out.

From that dramatic moment until now, I've painfully and carefully crafted a new perspective for dealing with others. None of us can know the awesome power and impact of a single statement reaffirming our love, need, and approval of another human being. What a bargain price to pay for ensuring our relationships! Dare we risk living without it . . . for even one day?

Through the pages of this book, pursuit of a higher standard of living, leading, learning, and loving will be challenged. However, a far greater adventure awaits. We'll unlock a priceless-but-forgotten secret that will transform our relationships. It's like gold! It's free, and it's ours as we uncover the key to giving others the one thing they want most, but will never ask for! Discover how to awaken a new dimension of human expression and interaction. Read, absorb, and apply the principles here to win happier, healthier, and yes—*phenomenal* results for all your human encounters.

A Few More Calories, Please

After paying my membership fee to a high-class fitness center, I was ready for my initial workout. Determined to shed those pesky, paunchy pounds, I headed for the weightroom. First, I was detoured to a small room resembling a doctor's office. Here, the counselor plugged electrodes to my limbs while beeps and blinking lights danced across a computer screen.

Minutes later, I received a printout detailing my ideal weight, total body fat, metabolic rate, and the number of calories needed to maintain my present weight. The idea, of course, was to consume less, so that there would be less of me.

Our human need for approval and appreciation is strikingly similar! We require praise in much the same way that our bodies consume calories. Basic human needs are organized in two levels. At the *primary* level are our drives for breath, thirst, hunger, sex, rest, shelter, and protection. When there is no bread, we exist for bread alone. Meanwhile, our needs for love, status, and recognition lie dormant.

Once the primary drives are reasonably satisfied, needs at a *secondary* level begin to emerge—demands for belonging, acceptance, friendship, love, approval, achievement, and self-esteem.

For most of us, the primary needs are more than satisfied. We live comfortably and eat three meals a day—whether we need them or not. It is our *secondary* needs that often present the greatest challenge.

We quickly realize that a person suffering from a dietary deficiency is unhealthy. Lack of proper nutrients brings on physical and behavioral problems. Similar consequences surface when higher level needs are lacking. Without these, we are ailing as though suffering from disease. And our illness will result in negative behaviors.

Victims suffering starvation continue to expend calories at an adequate rate to maintain life. When food fuels are exhausted, fatty tissues, muscle, and lean tissues are gradually consumed. In the terminal stages of starvation, even vital organs are ravaged in a desperate attempt to preserve life. Death comes only after the body has made every effort to maintain its existence.

Realize our need for approval is as essential as air, food, and water!

The will to live prevails in most of us. But when we fail to maintain the usual amount of human affirmation, we begin to exhibit distress, depression, and even physical illness.

Continual negative behavior patterns are usually noticed by caring friends who may inquire, express concern, or offer help. Such "strokes" revive our spirits and we recover. Without them, we may die psychologically in a manner much like physical death by starvation.

Think for a minute. What are you most likely to do when you feel depressed?

Oprah Winfrey once admitted, "Whenever I feel low, I reach out and touch someone, just like the commercial says. I call my best friend."

Most of us do the same. Talking with another human provides the stroking, the recognition, the warmth, and the interaction necessary to resurrect our spirits.

Just as we devour food on a daily basis, we are consumers of praise in a similar manner. Applause lasts for a brief interval. Then we require a fresh supply. Just as we wake up thinking, *What's for breakfast?*, our spirits are searching for the daily diet of recognition necessary to validate our existence.

"Three billion people on earth go to bed hungry every night, but *four billion* people go to bed every night hungry for a simple word of encouragement and recognition," says public speaker Cavett Roberts (Zig Ziglar, *Top Performance*, Revell, 1986).

Is feeding the hungry one of your priorities? Make a difference in someone's life today by satisfying primary or secondary needs.

Pass them just a few more calories, please!

For the Life of You!

"When I told my mother I had AIDS, she told me, 'You deserve it. You deserve to die,'" recalled a client at Houston's Bering Care Center. "When they first come here," he explained, "people are broken-hearted. Everything in your life is gone—your future has been taken away from you. And no one understands what you're going through."

With his comments fresh in my mind, I half expected the somber mood of a mortuary as I approached Bering Care Center.

"They must be having a birthday party," I mused while entering amid sounds of laughter and animated conversation.

Who would think this could be a happy place? Bering is a day care center for people with AIDS. Nothing to be happy about here, right?

Wrong.

Make a living by
what you get.
Make a life by what you give.

A letter to me from coordinator Patrick Richoux explains the reason behind the prevailing upbeat, positive mood in his center:

I believe praise is the most important thing we do for our clients here! Most of them have been rejected by family, friends, and society in general because they have AIDS. Consequently, they have an extremely low self-image, which in turn causes most of them to suffer from clinical depression. Over and over I've seen how just a little praise and approval has enabled clients who had given up on life to come around and become active volunteers at the center. At first, we could never get them to assist in the smallest tasks—like setting the table or washing the dishes. But after consistently receiving praise, they often take the initiative and volunteer to help. And it doesn't have to be a big deal—just praise for their efforts to come to the center or a comment on how good they look today will work wonders. As a result, they encourage other depressed clients to get on with living in a positive way!

Richoux wisely realizes how powerfully praise affects everyone. It's uplifting! Praise reaches avenues that medicine cannot travel. By transforming attitudes and building self-esteem, praise revives hope within the spirit. With renewed will to live, the life expectancy of Richoux's clients increases. To restore one's faith in one's self is to perform miracles!

While this book will spotlight praise in leading, learning, and loving situations, no activity is so basic as *living*. As early as childbirth, after a long, hard passage into daylight, stroking assured us that life in the cold, harsh world would be okay. Human reassurance was life-giving then—just as it is now!

A phenomenal, unexplainable, almost mystical reaction is triggered in the human spirit through an injection of PraisePower. It transmits a healing balm;

soothes wounded emotions; and resurrects the lonely, depressed, and dejected. From birth to death, praise is always appropriate, always needed, always welcome—and always certain to create positive results.

It is easy to become so engrossed in our business of making a *living* that we neglect to make a *life*. Unselfishly giving ourselves to others produces those rich, life-making experiences. Exercise your PraisePower to transform the lives and circumstances of others. While we make a living by what we *get*, let us reach for a new dimension of human expression as we make a life by what we *give*.

So You Wanna Win the Lottery?

"Oh, my God. Oh, my God!" Leslie gasped as he clutched the winning ticket in the Wisconsin lottery. "I had a hard time convincing Colleen that I wasn't pulling her leg. She tried to check the numbers and eventually had to grab the ticket from me because I was shaking."

Just how does it feel to hit the jackpot? Leslie Robins, Wisconsin high school English teacher, should know. Robins and his fiance won a record $111 million, netting the largest sum ever collected by a single player in the history of U.S. lotteries.

In spite of his record winnings, Leslie Robins made what many would consider an unusual decision. He chose to continue his job as a teacher, earning a $30,000 annual income. Why would he do that when he could enjoy anything money can buy?

"It may sound corny to some," Robins explained as he recalled letters of thanks he had received from former students. "You can't replace those letters with any amount of money!" he declared.

If only I could win the mega-million-dollar lottery! Or get that call from Ed McMahon! We all dream for ways and means to become richer.

GREAT NEWS! You are richer than you ever dreamed! You are wealthier than all lottery winners combined. You have resources that Ed McMahon and his sweepstakes can never offer!

Each of us is endowed with a bank of unlimited funds from which to give and give—and keep on giving. A "currency" is available to purchase what dollars cannot. And the spender is left far wealthier than before he spent.

What is this currency?

It's the gift that Leslie Robins declared more valuable than his $111 million prize! It's the trophy that Louise Peattie terms the "golden coin" of praise. (*Good Housekeeping*, October 1950.)

Check your pockets now. Dig deep into your soul to discover pocketfuls ready for indulging others. Jingle and recall the coins of this currency that you have received. How does it feel to have your hard work and efforts noticed and admired? You wouldn't think of accepting payment, yet you feel reimbursed!

Invest in the happiness
of others.
Spend freely from the
riches within you.

Every human encounter offers a challenge for exercising your powers of appreciation. Place yourself in the shoes of another person for only a few seconds. Suddenly, you feel new understanding and empathy. At that moment, your response flows naturally. Warmed by the bond of humanity, something flows between the two of you, quietly gracing both participants. What is it? The golden coin of PraisePower!

In the rough and rowdy days of the 1849 California gold rush, popular trouper Lotta Crabtree sang and danced by the campfire flicker to entertain weary miners. Grateful listeners often tossed nuggets of pure gold at her feet!

When artists perform today, we offer more sophisticated recognition. Still, it is a shining response. By comparison, most of us play far more monotone roles in life. We are programmed to expect no applause for our modest contributions. Yet we eagerly clutch the "golden coin" when it is tossed in our direction!

Each of us yearns for praise, often subtly fishing for compliments. Why do we do this? It is essential for each of us to feel valued by others. We expect praise will make us feel the glow of their approval. And most often, it does.

In the December 1985 issue of *Redbook,* Ellen McGrath, Ph.D., states:

Appreciation is one of the basic human needs. We need to feel known, acknowledged, valued. It's what keeps us going. The need begins soon after birth. When we take our first step, ride our first bike, finish the peas on our plate, we want someone to applaud our achievements.

We don't stop needing appreciation when we're the ones serving those peas or showing someone else how to pedal. Appreciation boosts our spirits, builds our self-esteem, and makes us feel good—about ourselves and the people we love.

Entertainer Bob Hope understands the magical power of appreciation. Says Hope, "There is no more rewarding experience in life than doing something that adds to the happiness of others. You like to know when you hit the target. You may have aimed to do something generous or kind or needed, but did you succeed? How can you be sure you did unless the individual tells you or shows you?" (*Good House-keeping,* May 1955).

Can we place a dollars-and-cents value on praise? It is not possible. Its effect on the human spirit comes without a price tag—more valuable than the shining nuggets prized by the California miners.

PraisePower is GOLD that lies within us—untapped veins of the purest form ready for mining!

"He who praises another, enriches himself . . ." explained George Matthew Adams. "The poorest human being has something to give that the richest could not buy." Still it is a voluntary offering. None can extract its payment from an unwilling miser.

How about a spending spree of the most rewarding kind? Forget the lottery. At your disposal is a budget of unlimited funds—*genuine* funds that compelled millionaire Leslie Robins to keep his teaching job in spite of his new-found fortune! The more you spend, the more there is available. Why would any of us ever be stingy?

Jingle this wealth freely in your pocket, and at your next encounter, lavish it generously. Invest in the happiness of others. Spend freely from the riches within you. In so doing, you will become a master—not a miser—at practicing the power of praise!

Roots of Grace and
a Tombstone to Live By

He was just one of countless black Americans who felt the sting of racial prejudice. His grandmother was born a slave. His blacksmith grandfather was never permitted to own land. His brother attended law school in a university basement set apart for blacks.

In his quest to learn more of the family history heard at his grandmother's knee, Alex Haley set out to discover and create one of the classics of American literature. His unquenching search for truth carried him more than a half-million miles to authenticate his story—a bloody, horrendous trail that began with his great-great-great-great-grandfather, seized by slave traders along the shores of the West African Gambia.

George Haley, brother of the famous author, provided some insight into Alex's adventure. Determined to relive the actual experience of his captive ancestors, Haley arranged for passage on a Liberian cargo ship sailing for port in the United States. Late each evening, he climbed down the endless metal rungs into the deep, dark cargo hull. Stripped to his underwear, he slept on his back on a bare plank every night of the ten-day voyage. Here, he envisioned the shrieks and suffering, human filth, raging fever, misery, and death endured by his ancestors.

His story paints a portrait of human suffering perhaps like no other in modern American literature. We visualize his family as they helplessly endured the flailing whips, chains, torture, and unspeakable human atrocities. Treated as mere livestock, they were sold at auction. Branded with searing irons, they became the property of wealthy planters. Their babies were snatched from their arms and sold as merchandise.

Has any black American of this generation felt a more acute sense for the human indignities suffered by his people? Perhaps not. Was he affected by it? Absolutely! His *Roots* is a product of the pain and anguish of his soul. Recalling his attempts to empathize with the suffering of the slaves, Haley admits there were occasions when he felt like "going back through history swinging an axe at the society that permitted slavery to happen."

Having known the terror of injustice so intimately, one might think Alex Haley would have become bitter, angry, and bent on revenge. Yet he did not. This gentle, gracious man remained unspoiled by the magnitude of his success.

Find the good and praise it!

Remembering his friend in a *Parade* magazine tribute, Lamar Alexander recalls, "I believe Alex was put on earth to teach the lessons of *Roots* and then left here for a while to remind us of other lessons."

Other lessons?

"My dear friend Alex used to say, 'Find the good and praise it.' He especially liked to say that to people who were busy finding everything wrong with

America," Alexander explained. "It was a powerful message coming from the grandson of slaves, . . . from the man who wrote *Roots*."

Haley often enjoyed recounting one of his favorite stories about John Newton, once a slave ship captain. Illustrating his own positive philosophy, Haley loved to recall how Newton became a Christian and later wrote one of the world's greatest hymns, "Amazing Grace" . . . that saved a wretch like me." In this miraculous story of Christian conversion, Alex saw the beauty of his lifelong creed: Look through all the bad and determine to "find the good and praise it!"

Alex Haley was a national treasure! But even more, he was a monument to every human who has ever felt the pangs of human injustice. With book sales exceeding 6 million copies in 30 languages, Haley could have built a powerful platform to crusade, accuse, and condemn. And he would have been justified in doing so.

There is a lesson here for all of us! We can become *bitter.* Or we can become *better!* It's our choice. Determine to be a crusader for what is good and right, rather than a condemner of what is wrong. How easy it is for us to become vehement condemners, especially when we have been unjustly victimized. Haley must surely have felt that too during his twelve-year research odyssey.

In February 1992, Alex Haley died, leaving us a priceless legacy in his book—but an even greater gift in his life! His *book* taught us to revere and appreciate our history. Yet his *life* taught us to avoid being controlled by those unjust tragedies and "find the good" to make the world a better place than we found it.

Haley was buried next to the front porch of his grandparents' Tennessee home within earshot of where his grandmother and great aunts first recounted their stories that became *Roots*. But his most important message was not included in the nearly 700 pages of his best-selling book. Rather, it is engraved in stone in one brief sentence as a perpetual reminder to generations who would follow.

Facing heavenward from the soft earth that gently holds his remains, a hewn stone tablet silently decrees—as though hailing an eleventh commandment: "Find the Good and Praise It."

Be a Pocket-Change Philanthropist

Repeat after me: "HEY!"

Go ahead. Do it. One more time as loudly as you can!

"HEY!!!"

Hear the echo of your voice? Can you recapture the sound of your words?

Of course not. Now *that's* the beauty of applause from your pen—rather than from your mouth. The fleeting echo of a verbal comment has vanished within seconds. Written praise, however, can be cherished and relived again and again—becoming a matter of record!

In August 1960, Dwight Wendell Koppes offered an article for *The Rotarian* magazine entitled, "Be a 4-Cent Philanthropist." Mr. Koppes maintained that one can enjoy the role of philanthropist for the price of a postage stamp. (Can you believe four cents would buy a stamp in 1960?)

Of all the gifts of praise you've enjoyed, which do you remember most? Chances are, at least some of them were appreciative words expressed in a letter, a card, or a handwritten note.

Written applause carries a special power all its own. It confirms that honesty and goodwill have exerted tangible, visible effort. It can be relished repeatedly, making the acknowledgment seem permanent and official.

Penned praise is often easier to accept. We can savor the flavor without distraction. It is not necessary to invent some socially acceptable response.

The moment belongs solely to the reader. And it is delicious!

Public speaker Jack Canfield describes his "warm fuzzy file" composed of letters, reviews, and notes of appreciation. Whenever he feels unappreciated or insignificant, he is rejuvenated by rereading excerpts from his special file (*Self Esteem and Peak Performance*, 1987).

PraisePower has potential in the world of commerce as well. Remember the last time you were displeased with a product or service? Did you fire off a searing, hostile letter practically igniting the paper?

It takes less time to write a letter of appreciation than one aimed at "burning" the person who did you an injustice. There are thousands who merit recognition compared with sparse few who warrant criticism.

Put it in writing!
Document your applause
for lasting effect.

It's easy to grow irate at an incompetent waiter, but do we write a note commending a *good* waiter? What about the postal carrier who daily brings our mail? . . . the police officer who guards our neighborhood? . . . the librarian who assists our research?

In the service industries, both complaints and commendations from customers are weighed heavily when reviewing employee performance. Have you any idea how much your note of praise may impact the lives (and pocketbooks) of the dozens of customer service employees you meet daily?

Sure, penning your praise requires more energy and more time than verbal applause, but it's worth the difference. Some pretty important people think so too—including George Bush. He possibly owes much of his political success to his penning practices. Throughout his career, Bush has followed many of his contacts with a gracious written compliment or note of applause. Friends and political allies are not the only recipients of his penned plaudits. Even political foes and total strangers have enjoyed the former President's applause. Imagine the surprise of the astonished person who received a cordial presidential note for lending Bush an umbrella during an unexpected downpour!

Is your opinion honest? Will it encourage someone who would otherwise go unnoticed? Put it in writing and spend a stamp on it. You have an enormous duty to do so!

Organize your action plan. Buy a book of first-class stamps, label it "for praise only," and date it. Target a dozen or more recipients you want to contact this month.

Next, write your first note. Applause for your spouse or parent could follow this pattern: "Thanks for all you do! I don't say this often enough, but I appreciate your love and consideration very much."

If you're feeling helplessly awkward, visit a greeting card shop. Inspiration will surely seize you there. Thousands of ready-made expressions for every possible occasion and emotion await your selection. You are certain to discover one that expresses your feelings precisely.

And while you're there, look around. An amazing thing will happen as you peruse! Specific names and faces from your circle of family and friends will leap out at you—folks you haven't thought about in awhile.

Now you're feeling the true spirit of the philanthropist! Why does the philanthropist give away more money in a minute than most of us earn in ten years? Now you know—at least on a pocket-change level!

Yes, buy the cards you're holding—the ones that "say it" just exactly right! Who says there has to be a specific occasion for sending a card and a personal message? Many cards feature a "just because" message. Sign them and send them before you change your mind. The only regrets you may feel later will come as a result of the card you *didn't* send.

Would you like to receive an unexpected, intimate message from your spouse, child, or friend? Well, they would like to get such a note from you! Do it now. Just one act will break an endless chain of non-action. How much better to write one note than to list thirty people you really ought to write this month.

In their best-seller *CareerTracking,* Jimmy Calano and Jeff Salzman underscore the basics of written acknowledgment. "There's no better way to build rapport than to remember people on birthdays, anniversaries, and big events. If you're really organized you can write a year's worth of cards in one evening. A few people in our company send us cards . . . it's not at all expected, and we think no less of those who don't do it. Yet we're only human, and the people who get our attention are more likely to be remembered."

True, the price of a first-class stamp has changed since Dwight Wendell Koppes wrote his article decades ago, but human relations have not. People *still* require recognition and appreciation. If we can provide that, new motivation is born within the heart of the discouraged and unappreciated. With renewed courage, they are empowered to try again and achieve.

Even with the price of postage escalating annually, mailbox philanthropy is still the bargain of the century.

Bestow a priceless gift that is worth everything. For mere pennies, dispense your own bit of good will in an envelope. Be a pocket-change philanthropist. We often claim there just isn't time for completing all our best intentions. "Happy is the person who discovers there isn't time left for *not* doing them!" explains Mr. Koppes.

Five minutes, a first-class stamp, and your personal expression can spark a brighter, richer life. Bestow your fortune on others. Cultivate a conscious awareness of the good around you. In spite of the bumper stickers that would have us believe otherwise, *good happens!* Lots of it. Look for it in the actions of others. Take out your ever-ready pen and document it.

Start now in the "write" direction!

Secondhand Stuff Is Better

Kathy was assigned to attend a week-long training session I was conducting. Bright and pretty, she was a veteran employee who had seen the company grow through a decade of difficult changes. Weary with the monotony of her ten-year duty, she was contemplating resignation. With bright eyes and excitement, she described future plans.

A few days later, I realized this was the same "Kathy" a manager and I had discussed over lunch only a week before. "She's the best employee I've got!" he bragged. "I've actually timed her, and she gets twice as much done as the fellows that work around her."

Unfortunately, Kathy's manager never felt it worthwhile to convey his approval to her.

Eagerly, I related to Kathy her manager's admiration. Her eyes brimmed over with tears. "Really?" she whispered in disbelief. "I never would have guessed he felt that way."

A most gratifying kind of applause to give or receive involves a comment relayed to you by someone else who heard it. Norman Vincent Peale admits that repeating a secondhand compliment is his favorite hobby.

How does he do it? "I've trained myself to listen," confides Dr. Peale, "for any word of approval or praise that one individual speaks about another—and to pass it on" (*Reader's Digest*, June 1972). What a simple yet powerful idea! Pass it on the next time you meet the person who was complimented. Everybody wins! The originator feels good for having said something positive. The recipient is rewarded happily and unexpectedly. And you, the person in the middle, witness the glow in the face of the recipient!

These mini "spirit-uppers" often strike their target at a time when the recipient needs it most. In the two years since hearing her manager's praise, Kathy's plans have changed. Remaining with the firm, she is pursuing a management career.

"When you hear something pleasant related to you about another person, you are being given a choice," explains Dr. Peale. "You can absorb it and let it stop right there—or you can deflect it to hit the real target. More than once I have used this ricochet principle successfully in dealing with some knotty tangle in human affairs."

Circulate all the good you hear about others.

Secondhand praise can be more significant than direct praise. Knowing that people are talking about you in a positive way is invigorating. Plus, you realize you're being told only a fraction of the actual conversation. Just imagining what else may have been said generates good feelings.

However, no one is suggesting that you should filter your own applause through a third party. If you have something praiseworthy to say, *you* should say it directly. Employ the secondhand approach to spread good will for others who may not have the courage, consideration or opportunity to praise directly.

In a decade when conservation and recycling are vital concerns, you'd think we'd work harder at preserving those precious yet perishable petals of praise. Start a recycling revolution! Circulate all the good you hear. Develop the practice of repeating any positive thing, any pleasant thing, any complimentary thing that you hear. The more often such little sparks of goodwill are recycled into the atmosphere, the less pollution of unhappiness and insignificance we suffer.

Two centuries ago, Benjamin Franklin was an advocate for recycling praise! "Speak ill of no man," wise Ben advised, "but speak all the good you know of everybody."

In Scripture, Saint Paul made a similar suggestion two millennia ago. "Finally, brethren," he summarized, "whatever things are true . . . ." He then added a catalog of positives including noble, just, pure, lovely, of good report. . . .

In climax, Paul stated, "*If there is anything praiseworthy,* meditate on these things" (Phil. 4:8). Bible scholars specify Paul's true intent: identify what is praiseworthy in others and *focus* on it.

Adopt this two thousand-year-old PraisePower principle. You'll discover it's just as relevant now as then!

How to Propel
Your Personal PraisePower

"Well, uhhh . . . I don't really know what to say . . .
I'm not very good with . . . Uhhh, you know how I
am . . . Well, anyway, I uh, this isn't coming out
right . . . If I could express what I really . . . It's just
not my . . . I've never been one with words . . . It's hard
for me to . . . Gee, what can I say?"

"I can't do that!" you protest. "It's just not 'me'
to say all those goody-goody things nobody believes
anyway."

No one wants to be a fraud and verbalize emotions
they don't really feel. But you *can* become proficient
in the art of sincere applause. Not only will it enrich
you emotionally, but there is an abundance of benefits to accompany your praise.

Employ the keys to
successful praising to enjoy
a key to successful living.

"Praise can help you establish rapport, cause
others to see you as warm and caring, build self-
esteem, and even change other people's behavior,"
says Donald Moine, Ph.D., in a recent issue of *Glamour* magazine. Now that's precisely the kind of power
we're talking about—propelling PraisePower! This is
not power for controlling the actions of others. It *is*
power transmitted to others for empowering their

own lives and actions. When skillfully delivered, praise works with almost everyone. Transform your human relations skills with the key PRAISE acronym! Personally pursue these proven pointers to propel your personal PraisePower!

Personalize!

For more emphatic applause, *personalize your praise*. Offer a comment to your recipient that is solely unique and original—something that would be inappropriate for anyone else. Start by using their name.

It appeals to our human nature to enjoy applause for something we are not normally known for achieving. When someone spotlights a little-known detail of our personality or ability, he is eternally our friend!

Just as surely as praise begins with the letter P, powerful praise begins by personalizing your plaudits. And it has potential for premiers and princes as well as paupers . . . for professors and principals as well as pupils . . . for priests and preachers as well as parishioners . . . for parents and partners as well as public and private persons. Well, you're getting the idea. Before we all "p-overdose," let's move on.

Recognize!

The entire premise of PraisePower is founded on your keen and timely ability to *recognize the good in others.*

The purest form of praise involves more than saying something nice. It employs the whole of you to be acutely tuned to the other person. Focused awareness is the key. Understand what motivates him and your efforts to praise will have meaningful significance.

Determine to recognize some unique facet you haven't noticed before. Some of the best qualities and strengths in each of us are often best-kept secrets. Look underneath the surface. Search deeper in less conspicuous places for strengths you can recognize and verbalize to others.

Offering applause to others because we feel we should is praising for the wrong reason. To get-out-there-and-praise-someone may be our personal goal, but it may not be what someone else needs at that moment. The highest affirmation we can offer is our awareness. When we are clearly focused on another person, we will not only recognize good when it happens, but we'll also get a feel for offering an appropriate response.

Analyze!

PraisePower requires you to *analyze your target* before you aim. Not everyone requires the same measure of praise. The art of personal praise involves determining how receptive your listener will be.

And as you start to praise, analyze your recipient's reaction. Respond to the feedback you're getting. Body language will provide you with plenty of clues. A smile is a positive sign. However, if your recipient begins shaking his head, grimacing, or avoiding eye contact, it may indicate an improper setting or expression. If so, back off gently.

A professor at a large university implores: "When

you compliment someone, you must not exceed that person's tolerance level. If you pour on too much, the person you're praising will think, 'That's not really me—that makes me feel like a phony.'"

Our individual tastes for recognition were patterned from childhood. If we get showered with more praise than our comfort zone allows, we shy away uneasily.

When you praise a person with low self-esteem, you must be especially sensitive. When receiving praise for some quality we don't believe we possess, we often express shock, disbelief, or doubts in our admirer's judgment. Yet often the recipient's need for affirmation is strongest where he lacks self-esteem. It's a matter of matching style of praise to the style of person. Analysis requires entering another person's awareness. We call it empathy. By examining the whole person, we find clues as to what the person needs.

Improvise!

The only thing that feels better than applause is MORE applause! If your recipient's reaction is positive, maximize your PraisePower by extending the applause when the situation allows it. Grant him the luxury of savoring every sweet second of your attention.

How? *Improvise and intensify your praising.* Wing it!

You be the judge. As host of a dinner party, which of these comments would delight you more?

"Great meal!"

Or, "Lee, no one makes veal like yours! How do you always make it so tasty and tender?"

The latter statement invites a cordial response and extends your applause. Of course, you can't say it the same way every time. Cater to the mood of the moment.

Now *that's* where improvisation comes in! Maximize the moment when you recognize the feeling is right. Only you can know for sure when that will be.

Improvising also means sometimes you *don't*. Your responses will vary depending on the occasion and the reactions you're reading. In some cases, of course, praise should be quick. In every case, it should fit the occasion and the recipient.

The best of praise can sometimes be ruined by pressing for a verbal response. Don't require your recipient to reply immediately—or ever. Allow him the pleasure of responding (or not) in whatever form he chooses. After all, it's his gift!

Invite input. Inquire. Interview. Individualize. Improvise!

Specify!

Verbal applause should *be specific—not "terrific!"* An almost total lack of originality is what a couple of linguists found in their analysis of praise phrases. More than 40 percent of the comments included the words *good* or *nice*.

Too many of us who choose to praise do so by generalizing, a technique that dilutes the power from our praise. Vague terms show a lack of thought and creativity on the part of the praiser.

Mumbling "good job, guys" does not express approval. What kind of reward is that for a deserving employee? Specifics seem to validate the sincerity of our applause. Listen in on Sam praising his sales staff at their weekly meeting: "With the new accounts each of you has added this month, we have exceeded our quotas by twenty percent! Now that's phenomenal effort, and you are responsible! My sincere thanks!"

Simple? Yes, but small details pay big dividends. Qualify your praise with specifics for maximum effect!

Express-ercise!

The more you exercise a muscle, the more powerful it grows. Same thing happens with your PraisePower. Master a new art form of interpersonal relations—*express-ercise. Exercise your right to expressive praise!*

Implement a human relations routine with the same vengeance you exert in your physical workout. Make it your conscious, daily habit to look for the good in others and to proclaim your discoveries!

It takes *all* of the keys mentioned here to achieve maximum results. If any onx of thxsx six xlxmxnts is lxft out, your praisx will not bx as xffxctivx as it could bx! Sxx how onx small, inactivx kxy affxcts this xntirx paragraph? The othxr twxnty-fivx kxys arx working propxrly. The samx thing can limit your praisx. Implxmxnt all thx kxy xlxmxnts for maximum praisx powxr! Xxprxss-xrcisx! Xxpress-xrcisx! Xnjoy! Xnjoy!

In summary, let's reappraise our PRAISE:

Personalize. Attempt to say something solely unique, original, and appropriate that distinguishes your recipient from all others.

Recognize. Learn to recognize the good in others. Seek to identify specific strengths and positives through deliberate, focused awareness.

Analyze. Before you aim, analyze your target. Tailor your praise to fit your recipient. As you praise, analyze any reaction—positive or negative.

Improvise. Wing it! Improvise, maximize or adjust your praise based on the feedback you're getting.

Specify. Be specific—not "terrific!" Avoid generalities and vague, trite phrases.

Express-ercise. Exercise your right to expressive praise. Make it your conscious, daily habit to look for the good in others and proclaim your discoveries!

Inner Space:
The Next Frontier!

"Houston, Tranquility Base here. The Eagle has landed." It was one for the history books! On July 20, 1969, the United States Apollo spacecraft settled onto the lunar surface.

Immeasurable time, expense, and human lives have been dedicated to space exploration since that day. Man has touched the moon. Men and women have walked and worked in space free of the limitations of gravity. Satellites orbit our earth as you read. Aeronautics has soared beyond our level of comprehension.

We cheer the efforts to further probe the mysteries of outer space. Yet, there awaits a far greater galaxy to be fully explored—*inner space!* What is it within each earthling that thrusts us to reach for out-of-this-world results? What is it that ignites our will and propels us to soar beyond our limits? Why is it that too many of us never get off the ground despite talent and ability?

As inner space explorers, that's what our flight plan is set to reveal in this book.

Suppose you offered a word of praise to two people today. Then each of them uttered a similar kindness tomorrow. If the process continued, one hundred twenty people would feel the magic of praise within one week! If the cycle continued, sixteen thousand people would be affected within two weeks. In just three weeks, *two million* persons would be touched by praise!

Praise is powerful! But praise is not the ultimate be-all, end-all, cure-all for the world's ills. It never will be. It will, however, vastly improve the quality of living for you and those you touch. It is from this perspective that we learn together about praise—the crown jewel of all interpersonal relations!

Stepping onto the moon's surface, Neil Armstrong summarized the vast achievement: "That's one small step for man, one giant leap for mankind."

Your efforts at praising may seem insignificant, a "small step" for you, but the prospects for changing another life qualify as a "giant leap for mankind." Break through the sound barrier that has muzzled your praise too long!

Countdown to a new adventure in human relations! . . . Ten . . . nine . . . eight . . . seven. . . . All systems are go! . . . Six . . . five . . . four . . . . Ignite your good intentions to action! . . . Three . . . two . . . one. . . . Lift off!

Accelerate your PraisePower toward this noble frontier: inner space. Your launch will find smooth landing on a higher, happier plane of living!

TWO

Pursue a Higher Standard of Leading

The greatest good we can do for
others is not to share our riches
with them, but to reveal
theirs to them.

Chapter Objectives

○ Adopt a head-and-heart approach to leadership.

○ Remember, your praise is worth more than $$$.

○ Empathize. What you want is what *they* want.

○ Speak up! Tell them when they're doing okay.

○ Make it your business to take care of your people, and your people will take care of your business.

○ Make listening your *first* choice at a *second* chance.

○ Be there to witness and applaud achievements as they happen.

○ Be contagious! Start a praise epidemic with your boss.

○ Make your people your partner. Allow them to see and feel the human side of you.

○ Make "thank you" a part of your working vocabulary.

○ Pinpoint and proclaim the positives in your people.

○ Embellish your praise with frequent gold stars.

○ Credit your vital-but-not-visible support staff.

○ Look for the best *in* them to get the best *out* of them!

○ Appraise your applause.

○ Learn to accept praise graciously.

You want to be a successful leader?

Sure.

How successful?

You haven't given it much thought?

Then close this book and give it to one of your more ambitious friends.

You're still reading. Then you *are* interested in effective leadership. You *do* want to be a climb-to-the-top-of-the-ladder kind of achiever! You hunger for that how-on-earth-did-she-do-it kind of success!

As a busy professional, you want to make the most of your time and resources. Thousands of books published this year are screaming to be read. No writer can expect you to read his book unless there's something in it for you—like the secret to successful leadership just mentioned.

Well, you *can* have it! The secret lies in doing the little things the other corporate climbers don't, like taking care of your staff. If you nourish your team as outlined in the following pages, not only will you be a success, your people will *carry* you to the top on their shoulders!

And along the way, you will enjoy benefits known to only a handful of successful leaders. While most corporate scramblers are burning their energies to "make it" on their own, you will be riding to success—fueled by the cooperation and loyalty of your own team!

Now, back to the question. What's in it for you?

Your Job Will be Easier

 . . . with fewer problems, less stress, fewer complaints. Sounds like a dream? It probably is—unless you begin to apply the principles suggested here.

Each time friction erupts within a team, precious time is wasted. Efficiency and productivity take a nosedive. By developing good working relationships, routine operations will hum along smoothly while productivity and quality soar!

You'll Enjoy Respect, Cooperation and Loyalty

. . . by taking the effort to build a sincere relationship with your staff. It doesn't require an M.B.A. or a diploma in how-to-make-people-feel-good to understand basic principles of human relations.

It is one matter to have things go well. It is a different matter entirely to appeal to your staff and watch them expend extra effort for you. Such leadership spells the difference between modest success and a brilliant victory!

Empathize with your people. For whom would you work harder: A manager whom you respect and admire? Or one who has been careless and distant with you? Of course, you *know* the answer to that question!

Your Reputation and Your Career Will Soar

. . . while you help your people grow. "There is something rarer than ability," explains Robert Half. "It is the ability to recognize ability" (*Management Without Tears*, Crain Books, 1981).

Your efforts will not go unnoticed! You're grooming your staff for success and for the realization of their own career goals. As someone who develops people and achieves results, you will become a tangible benefit to your organization. And guess who gets the nod next time promotions are discussed?

You Will Look Good

. . . because of your sincere, deliberate efforts to provide meaningful, positive support.

How does it happen? Your sincerity breeds cooperation . . . which builds teamwork . . . which increases quality and productivity . . . which fosters a sense of pride in what your team is doing!

All of these results show up directly on the bottom line of the operating statement . . . and you will look good—because you will be!

Now isn't this where you really wanted to be all along—stepping *up* the corporate ladder rather than standing *under* it?

Missing the Mark
by Eighteen Inches

Would *you* work for this man? As surviving owner of the Scrooge & Marley Company, he projected a hardnosed, "bah humbug" attitude toward everybody and everything!

The stereotypical manager of yesteryear depicted in the Charles Dickens classic strikes fear in all of us. To this insensitive dictator, employees had no faces, feelings or personalities. They existed solely as manpower to rake in greater revenues for the boss.

Today's training, sophistication, and awareness have made Mr. Scrooge almost extinct. He represents the caveman mentality that we hope is gone forever.

The modern leader must possess qualities never experienced by prehistoric management. His role remains in flux and he must learn to continually adapt.

For generations, the university schools of business have perfected the executive art. Technology and sophistication have sculpted the ultimate manager. Fresh off the assembly line, these cookie-cutter clones are fine-tuned in the textbook art of management. They've learned to "do things right."

In their captivating book *Leaders,* Warren Bennis and Burt Nanus state the key difference between leaders and managers in a brief but brilliant summary: "Managers do *things right,*" they declare. "Leaders do the *right thing.*"

Strictly by-the-book process produces managers who are well-versed in the theory of leadership. While marginally successful, many managers progress no further. It's in their *heads*—but not in their *hearts*. They are missing the manager's mark by eighteen inches!

Thus emerges another organ equally important in the art of people management! Providing meaningful feedback and appreciation requires unique qualities of the heart.

Applauding performance demands the skill of evaluating people according to their own abilities. When appraising people by corporate standards, it is easy to overlook how phenomenal their achievements are *for them!*

Approval and respect are two of the most valuable but rarest commodities in today's workplace. Why? The only way to *get* them is by *giving* them away! If you are not enjoying the validation and respect you would like, it may be that you are managing by head and not by heart. A higher standard of leadership employs a delicate balance of both.

Adopt a head-and-heart approach to leadership.

At some point along the way, managers grabbed the notion that intimidation, fear, and coercion equalled productive leadership. True, such tactics can be effective for the short term! You can motivate people by threatening them with their jobs. But you will never compel them to care about you or your business.

If the ability to inflict raw will on workers resulted in a measure of productivity, the defunct Soviet Union would have reigned as a champion exporter in global markets. The total collapse of their political, governmental, and economic systems is glaring proof that sheer force is an ineffective stimulant.

The productive worker must be motivated by other means. One of the most valuable—yet least used—modes is sincere recognition. In short, PraisePower! Why is it that some managers are able to get phenomenal performance while others struggle to meet minimum standards? Why do some coaches produce winning teams year after year while others experience only sporadic success?

The answer points to the leader's ability to inspire greater performance. As manager, your success depends on your ability to get things done through other people. The moving, driving, burning spirit you need in your team comes from the heart of the leader.

All of the business textbooks in the world cannot transmit that kind of leadership! In such moments, theory takes a back seat. Management-by-heart scores a shining victory that textbook ideology alone cannot duplicate.

A basic principle in balancing the head-and-heart management style is: companies produce nothing—people produce everything. An organization is successful only because the people within that unit are successful.

Managers in pursuit of a higher standard of leadership understand and implement management-by-heart. They recognize their most important asset is not necessarily housed in the cranium mounted on their shoulders. They know their employees. They are sensitive. They listen and respond to them. As a result, their teams achieve higher levels of personal success and develop a pattern of continual growth.

Here's the *heart* of the matter. As a leader, your expectations are never squandered on your staff. People have a way of soaring (or sinking) to the level set for them. Exhibit faith in their ability and soon they too believe. That's what PraisePower is all about— empowering others to a new, enlightened awareness and rediscovery of their own strengths and talents!

Managers who expect greater performance *receive* more. Teachers who set higher standards *see* higher grades. Coaches who envision more victories *win* more games.

Why? Because their expectations are honest and sincere. They manage in the warmth of this faith. The eighteen inches between their head and heart is a well-worn path! They transmit their heartfelt convictions, and their team is inspired to higher levels of performance than they ever dreamed possible!

How to Keep Them "I-Would-Do-Anything-for-My-Boss!" Kind of Happy

While lunching at a cafeteria recently, I overheard four young women seated at the table next to mine.

"Can you believe," one of them gasped, "he actually gave us a compliment?"

"I thought he would choke first," another one quipped.

"Didn't think it would happen in my lifetime!" chirped another.

And the fourth response? Well, let's just say it wasn't print worthy.

Unfortunately, the plight of this quartet of young professionals is far too common. Sociologists Ronny Turner and Charles Edgley reported out of 245 observed instances of praise, only 8 percent occurred in the workplace.

PraisePower is the most positive generator accessible to you as a leader. It is simple, inexpensive and available in inexhaustible supply. Surprisingly, it is also the least used. It's the sure-fire way to keep them "I-would-do-anything-for-my-boss" kind of happy. As a motivator, praise is matchless. It's the one thing they want *most* but will *never* ask for! The myth still exists in leadership circles that money is the almighty motivator. Too many surveys indicate the contrary. Praise from someone in authority, who commands respect and admiration, is often a stronger motivator than a pay raise. Regardless of how outstanding our performance is, promotions come along infrequently. But any manager can reward an employee by simply voicing praise when it is deserved.

The *Advanced Management Journal* published a study concluding that the average employee considers "full appreciation of work done" a top priority. Polling both workers and their managers, the study revealed some other surprises.

Managers seemed appalled that their subordinates were *most* interested in recognition. Wages, security, promotions, and favorable working conditions were the amenities managers ranked highest.

"If I tell them they're doing a good job, they'll be asking for more money!" one manager protested. Actually, when leaders develop the verbal applause habit, the number of employees asking for raises diminishes.

Remember, your praise is worth more than $$$.

Sure, some wise guy may quip, "I want my appreciation spelled out on my paycheck." But the majority of your troops will glow and thrive under the warmth of your applause.

Once an aspired standard of living is achieved, each of us tends to focus our energy toward realizing other goals. Respect, recognition, job satisfaction, and the approval of our peers become conscious goals.

The wise manager realizes the needs of his team members for achieving these non-monetary goals. A skillful bouquet of verbal roses-not-raises helps make this happen.

No one has measured the maximum potential of human beings. We do know that even the most dedicated worker rarely exceeds 15 to 20 percent of his brain capacity in a day's labor. The average worker can easily double, even triple, his efficiency.

What would happen if managers changed their mind-set and began to manage in terms of doing things *for* their staffs instead of doing things *to* them? Productivity would soar off the charts!

We exert enormous energy in proving our importance to our peers. It's human nature. What do leaders do? The same thing! They expand the size of their offices, their staff, their territory, and their authority. Sure, money is an important reward, but primarily people want to be treated special in order to feel special about themselves.

Subordinates feel the same way. They try to win the applause of others if only because, when others accept them, they can finally begin to accept themselves.

Tim, owner of a small graphics firm, shares a roses-not-raises principle for successful leadership: "I've made it my goal to find some sort of event to celebrate at least once a week. The occasion is usually not a big deal—at least not expensive. More often it may be kolaches and coffee. The focus is not on the details but on the people. Oh boy, do we celebrate! . . . and boy, do I celebrate every time I look at the books and see how well we've done this year!"

Most of us work for love and money. Few of us ever get our fair share of either. Assign top priority to building up your team and enjoy phenomenal results. It will only happen by doing the *big* things—like empowering your staff through PraisePower. And the *little* things—like kolaches and coffee.

Is What We Want What They Want?

In 1989, Louis Harris & Associates surveyed office employees and managers of a prominent office furniture company. Their research found an expanding "perception gap" between what workers really want and what top administration *thinks* they want.

So, what did they want? Was it higher wages? . . . better working conditions? . . . more benefits?

Would you believe that none of these topped the list of employee wants?

Managers assumed that job security was the prime concern to employees. Among workers, however, job security ranked below such desires as respect, approval, increased recognition, and closer communication between employees and management (*Fortune,* December 4, 1989).

Charles M. Schwab was notorious for gaining more production from his furnaces than any other steel firm. Yet he paid wages no higher than his competitors. Instead, Mr. Schwab did something more creative. Whenever a crew produced an extraordinary amount of tonnage, Schwab made a deliberate visit to the furnace to thank that crew personally. His employees' response to his praise crowned him king of the steel industry.

"I consider my ability to arouse enthusiasm among the men the greatest asset that I possess, and the way to develop the best that is in a man is by appreciation and encouragement," explained Schwab. "There is nothing else that so kills the ambitions of a man as criticism from his superiors" (*The

Master Manager, John Wiley and Sons, 1980). To shatter the mighty money myth, co-author James Evered offers a brilliant analogy in his book *Shirt Sleeves Management:*

> Pick your favorite professional football team. Assume we offer each player a 20 percent increase in contract pay—with two restrictions: (1) absolutely no fans allowed in the stadium during the game, and (2) no press coverage during or after the game. How long would professional football last? It would die immediately. Why? Because we would have robbed them of their greatest motivation—the recognition that comes from achievement.

In 1988, Opinion Research Corporation of Chicago polled 100,000 employees of Fortune 500 companies from middle managers, professionals, and salespersons to technical, clerical, and hourly workers. Their findings only confirmed earlier surveys.

Empathize. What you want is what *they* want.

Employees overwhelmingly perceived top management to be less willing to listen to their problems than they were five years earlier. The same workers also felt less personal respect from their administration. Many "open door" corporations were found to have their doors only slightly ajar.

What do your employees *really* want? Figure 1

shows ten components used to measure employee concerns. On the left, rate the three most important to you. Review the list again and check the three on the right you perceive to be of greatest value to your employees.

What did you discover? Did you mark both columns identically? If you're like most managers, probably not.

But when employees were polled with the same wish list, their responses were almost identical to those given by managers.

What I Want:		What They Want:
	Favorable working conditions	
	Management's allegiance to workers	
	Job security	
	Understanding personal problems	
	Interesting, challenging work	
	Fair wages	
	Promotion opportunities	
	Fair discipline	
	Appreciation for job well done	
	Feeling "in" on company goals and directions	

FIGURE 1

Does this say something about human nature? It should. Regardless of which hat we wear—manager or the managed—we have the same basic needs and desires. Your staff wants the very same things you want! And, as the surveys indicate, appreciation and recognition crown our list of desires.

Should the effective manager hesitate one minute longer? A higher standard of leading calls the dedicated leader to a greater understanding: PraisePower is a key motivator—and that makes for a happier, better adjusted, more productive team!

"If You Don't Hear from Me, You're Doing Okay"

Rocky is a man of few words—few good words, that is. Manager of a large human resources division, he is strictly business. He operates by the no-news-is-good-news philosophy. When pressed by staff members about the quality of their performance, Rocky prides himself in responding, "If you don't hear from me, you're doing okay."

Far too many managers operate on this management-by-exception technique. Such a brush-off response deprives employees of precious feedback essential to staying motivated to do a better job. And it creates a negative work relationship. If we hear from the boss only when we've done something wrong, our relationship will never be positive, pleasant, or healthy.

Donald Petersen, former Ford chairman, developed the habit of writing positive notes to his staff on a daily basis. "The most important ten minutes of your day are those you spend doing something to boost the people who work for you," Petersen declares. "Too often we think, *I haven't said anything critical; why do I have to say something positive?* We forget that human beings need positive reinforcement—in fact we thrive on it!"

Lack of positive feedback and recognition directly affects the quality of your employees' performance. Nothing hurts more than being ignored. It's the ultimate insult!

If you meet their efforts with silence, employees

become careless and negligent. By setting clear goals and offering specific feedback and recognition, your team will feel more secure and in control.

Successful leaders keep their people fully informed—not only about their performance, but also about current projects, upcoming activities, and the direction of the company. The wisest policy is to offer your workers *all* the information they might be interested in knowing. Hiding details only breeds suspicion, distrust, and a hotbed of rumors. Keep them so well informed that rumors don't have a chance.

You like to be in on what's happening, don't you? It feels good when the boss takes you into his confidence and updates you on vital concerns. When he doesn't, you feel somewhat slighted, less enthusiastic, and maybe even uncooperative. Why would the people who work for you feel any differently?

Practically every employee (including you) desires to do a solid job for his boss. Withholding feedback until something goes wrong damages your relationship with your employee. Emotions run high, tempers erupt, egos are crushed—causing employee confidence and productivity to plummet. Crisis management tactics often bring on numerous stress-related physical, mental, and emotional illnesses.

There is no justification for such waste. Avoid this management tragedy by regularly making the effort to discuss requirements, expectations, and evaluation of job performance.

Remember *your* first day on the job? Filled with fresh enthusiasm, you craved acceptance. Recall even the slightest indications your boss was pleased with your performance. How did you feel? Accepted? Relieved? More confident?

Why don't managers make better use of this valuable and inexhaustible commodity? There are many reasons.

For many of us, approval is a foreign language. Not knowing the joy of applause firsthand, we tend to discredit its value.

The pattern possibly began to develop from our earliest childhood experiences. When we smeared pudding or strained squash all over ourselves, our moms quickly told us how messy we were. Our housekeeping habits sparked a similar response. Parents denounced our sloppy rooms but never seemed to notice when things were cleaner than usual.

Well-meaning parents were sure their rebukes would make us improve. But little, if any, permanent modification occurred by reminding us we were making a mess, acting childishly, or being too noisy.

Internalizing our parents' critical approach, we now operate in the same way. We acquired critical habits in the formative years as teachers and parents continually pointed out defects. As adults, we now have learned to deal with others in the same manner we were treated.

Because we are critical of self, we are typically critical of others. We expect them to achieve *our* own performance standards. Like our parents, we note and denounce their every mistake and defect. So the vicious, destructive cycle perpetuates.

Managers may be reluctant to offer praise for another haunting reason. What if it is misplaced approval? What if the task our worker has completed isn't quite as good as it appears? He certainly won't protest our praise, but will he go off chuckling at our hasty appraisal? We feel safer in offering no comment.

Or it may be that, as manager, you are hesitant about playing a role that feels manipulative—somewhat like the motivational promoter who is always patting people on the back. Yet there is no act involved in praising the work of a deserving employee. If you and your staff enjoy a trusting relationship, there is nothing phony about saying, "You really came through for us, Bill!"

Speak up! Tell them when they're doing okay.

Then there are those who fear the awful truth: managers *do* need workers! Applauding workers on the quality of their performance may imply a manager's dependency on them. Insecure or cocky managers may balk at praise for fear it casts them to the mercy of their subordinates.

The confident and competent leader is not threatened by such an obvious fact. Yes, he *does* need his workers. His constant awareness secures the bond he has forged between himself and his staff. If approval is never voiced, workers soon recognize that good performance ranks equally with poor performance.

Anxious that fresh enthusiasm might reflect badly on them, veteran employees may exert subtle influence on new hires to perform at a lackluster level. If no recognition is offered for extra effort, such peer pressure often prevails. The manager then wonders what happened to that energetic, new-hire zeal. Such second-rate management becomes a breeding ground for mediocre performers.

It's a lose-lose situation. The manager and the employees all lose. Does anyone benefit? Sure! Your better-managed competition!

Your employees' fervor will never be as high as yours. Remember, you're the motivator. We're talking about a higher standard of leading! Can you realistically expect them to exceed *your* level of enthusiasm and passion for the job?

If you conceal your applause behind "If-you-don't-hear-from-me-you're-doing-okay," your staff will run for cover behind their "Nobody-cares-if-I-do-a-good-job" kind of indifference. They *must* know when their performance is exceptional. Let them hear you say it.

Initiate a new philosophy that demonstrates: "You'll *definitely* hear from me when you're doing okay!" Nothing you do will reap greater rewards. Go ahead. Now is the time to climb up to a new dimension of human expression.

Win the Malcolm Baldrige the "Overnight" Way

During his undergraduate days at Yale, Fred Smith submitted a term paper detailing his idea for an airline strictly for packages. Neither he nor his economics professor could have realized the impact his notion would have on the global business structure. Smith's professor awarded him a grade of C. The corporate world, however, has been a bit more responsive to Smith's unique idea.

When Federal Express opened for business in April 1973, it boasted an eight-plane fleet and shipped eight packages the first night. Its humble beginnings hailed more than the birth of a company—rather the threshold of a new industry: overnight air express, transforming the way the world does business.

In 1983, Federal Express made history by becoming the first U.S. company to exceed one billion dollars in revenues within its first decade. It has grown to annual revenues of more than seven billion dollars and retains a 43 percent market share of the air express market. Almost 100,000 employees in 200 countries move 300 million packages annually. With a fleet of more than 430 aircraft, Federal Express now commands the largest air cargo line in the world. How did all of this happen so quickly? Take note of yet another stellar accomplishment. In 1990, Federal Express was named recipient of the Malcolm Baldrige National Quality Award, representing the highest distinction for quality within an American company. Federal Express was the first service company ever to be awarded the Baldrige trophy (from *Aviation and Space Technology,* October 22, 1990).

Quality. Quality. Quality. The "Big-Q" has become the battle cry of American business. Weary of watching the Japanese capture many of our own markets, American companies are duplicating the Japanese emphasis on quality. Nearly every major corporation is now singing the "Big-Q" hit song. Millions of corporate dollars are being funneled into consultants, personnel, training, and quality control programs.

However, Fred Smith believes the *real* key to quality success lies in a commodity your company already possesses—your *people.* Smith's conviction is engraved in the simple, three-word corporate philosophy that governs his international organization: People-Service-Profit. In that order.

"When people are placed first," explains Smith, "they will provide the highest possible service, and profits will follow."

Make it your business to take
care of your people, and
your people will take care
of your business.

To enact their philosophy, Federal Express has designed several effective tools to demonstrate that employee opinions *do* matter and ideas *are* welcome. One of the most impressive is Survey-Feedback-Action, a unique exercise to promote dialogue between work groups and management.

Each spring, all employees complete a detailed "report card" evaluation of their manager's performance. Input is kept confidential. Yet survey results are weighed heavily in the corporation's appraisal of its individual managers. Follow-up involves a formal action plan for solving problems identified in the survey.

One statement to which employees are asked to respond reads: "My manager tells me when I do a good job."

The total work force surveyed in 1993 indicated an incredible 75 percent favorable response!

Another statement included in the survey declares: "My manager treats me with respect." Employees agreed with a resounding 85 percent positive reply.

Could there be a direct link between the strong-felt presence of management-employee appreciation and the phenomenal success achieved by this young corporation?

Fred Smith thinks so. "Our customer's perception of quality is in the hands of our people," Smith states convincingly. "Customer satisfaction begins with employee satisfaction. Buildings, equipment, and products don't make a company successful. People do!"

"The only edge you have now," echoes a consultant, "is with your people—quality of product is being superseded by quality of relationship, and that requires a very different way of running an organization."

The modern manager in quest of quality must learn the value of shifting the emphasis from his products to his people. The successful leader believes that if he takes good care of his employees, they in turn will take good care of his business. And "good care" includes voicing approval when it is warranted.

"As we expand internationally, we've found that the central idea of our people philosophy translates well," explains Smith. "Culture and language may differ, but from everything we've seen, human nature is universal."

By adopting the human approach, Federal Express beacons a new passage for all in quest of corporate quality. Creating the "perfect product" is no longer good enough. Today's business success demands that the leader relate to his customers and employees in such a way that his *people*—not his *product*—become the reason for his *profits!* (from *The Human Side of Quality,* Federal Express, August 1990).

Eavesdropping in the Washroom Stalls

"Why didn't he tell me before now? . . ."

"If only I had known about this . . ."

"I just wish she'd hear me out on this one . . ."

"I guess what he really meant was . . ."

"If I just knew where I stood with him! . . ."

"She never heard a word I said! . . ."

"Are you kidding? No way he'll ever find out from me!"

Do you want to know what your subordinates are thinking? Do you have the courage to find out? Are you *sure?*

Conduct a stakeout in the washroom stalls. As the comments stated above may prove, your adventure can be painfully revealing. Yet you may learn more perched on a porcelain throne than settled in your plush, leather boardroom chair.

Why don't we develop more healthy, productive relationships in the workplace? Generally, we assume more than we should. As managers, we presume that our employees are aware of job expectations. We become so busy directing that we stop listening. The higher we climb on the corporate ladder, the more distance we create between ourselves and others. It is easy to become enchanted with our own methods to the exclusion of others. A one-person show may run for the short term, but eventually every manager requires the benefit of a healthy team effort.

A manager who is deaf to his workers soon learns they are reluctant to confide their ideas with him.

Even worse, no one is willing to relay the bad news to him either. And that can prove catastrophic!

We must demonstrate to our staff that we *welcome* their feedback and ideas—the good, the bad, the terrible. Or we can always head for the washroom.

Overheard behind washroom doors, these candid expressions suggest the manager has failed to offer workers continual, clear feedback. He has forgotten that no one has a monopoly on good ideas—not even him. From his roost between the stalls, he discovers that his leadership ability is often questioned.

Some management concepts go without saying but *never* without listening. The most effective way to acknowledge your people is to include them in the day-to-day process of your business. Reacquaint yourself with your staff. Ask individual employees for their ideas and input on specific subjects. Talk to them, but start by *listening*.

Make listening your *first* choice at a *second* chance.

Employ these techniques for improving your listening skills so that the trip to the washroom won't be necessary.

- Look at your speaker. Maintain eye contact, yet be careful to avoid a hypnotic stare.
- Resist contemplating what your speaker will say next. Hear him out before drawing your own conclusions.

- Avoid interruption. Allow your speaker full and free expression.
- Keep an open mind. Ask fact-finding questions to clarify your perceptions.
- Listen to what you *can't* hear. Analyze nonverbal signals. Listen between the lines for hidden messages.
- Never allow your speaker's voice, mannerisms, appearance, or delivery to interfere with the content of the message. Evaluate the substance, not the speaker.
- Take a few good notes. Brief written phrases will tell your speaker that his responses are important to you.
- Resist emotional rebuttals. Don't allow emotionally charged words to rattle you. Maintain a calm, professional manner.
- Avoid external distractions through concentration. Pay your speaker the ultimate compliment by awarding him your undistracted attention.
- Maintain alert body language. Lean slightly toward the speaker to indicate your interest, yet be careful not to invade his "space."
- Listen for areas of common interest or agreement you can use to build a bridge of rapport and trust for future communications.
- Toward the end of your conversation, paraphrase what your speaker has said. "What I'm hearing you say, is . . ." Your verbal summary ensures clarity and confirms your alert attention.

Demonstrate to your staff that you welcome their input. But your success depends on more than just inviting it. Sure, it's easy enough to ask for feedback, but we're often emotionally attached to our own notions. Willingness to *implement* new ideas requires effort and commitment.

If you have governed the office with only your ideas in the past, don't expect the staff to be thrilled by your new all-ears policy. It will take time to earn their trust and confidence.

When your team realizes that you value their special talents and efforts, their creativity will astound you. They'll also start to feel they're an important part of your company and they will work harder to achieve its objectives.

With benefits like that, you can't afford *not* to make some changes in your management style. Start rebuilding your relationship today. Make listening your *first* choice at a *second* chance.

Far better to improve your listening skills with your staff than to find out the *hard* way—seated on the Great White Bowl.

Treat each of your employees to the dignity of one-on-one interaction. They deserve your attention or they shouldn't be working for you.

And please, move to a more comfortable chair!

The Hole-in-One That Nobody Saw

It was a lazy, overcast Monday morning. Grant drove to the golf course to play a solo round on his day off. His game went well . . . until he came to the sixth hole.

Pulling the three-iron from his bag, Grant took a couple of limbering practice swings and stepped up to the tee. Squinting at the target, he set his feet and rocked into a low backswing. Arms and club swung high, he uncoiled in a blur with a lightning explosion of power.

Whooooosh!

The sound was solid and perfect. The instant his club struck the ball, Grant *knew* it was a good one.

Higher, faster, farther! That streak of white arched and burst upward into the gray sky. Grant watched with satisfaction as the ball flew down the heart of the fairway and dived sharply onto the green almost two hundred yards away. This was one magnificent stroke!

Straining his eyes, Grant gasped in amazement as the tiny white speck rolled closer . . . closer . . . closer and . . . vanished into the cup! Grant was stunned. For an instant, all was silent in the cathedral of the green. Then, a roar went up from the gallery of one.

"Yessssssssss!" Grant yelled as he raced toward the flag, sending his three-iron flying. The echo of his voice boomed through the silent, wooded course.

"I don't believe it!" he kept shouting to no one in particular. The adrenaline rush made him delirious with excitement. "Wait till I tell the guys about this one!"

"Elated as I was," Grant explained later, "I felt an immediate sense of frustration. What if nobody believed me? How could I prove I really aced it? Ridiculous as it sounds, I wanted to take a picture of that ball in the cup! I can't tell you how hard it was for me to pick up the ball and move on."

Like Grant and his heart-breaking hole-in-one experience, our achievements are worth less—and enjoyed much less—if they go unrecognized by others.

Accepting and enjoying acknowledgment is a basic human need. We thrive on it and vie for it. Those who claim no interest in recognition or approval are either abnormal or fooling themselves.

> Be there to witness and
> applaud achievements
> as they happen.

Why else would we line our walls with trophies, plaques, and diplomas? These provide visible proof of our accomplishments. They validate our need for approval. It is our socially acceptable way of broadcasting our successes to others: "Look here, folks, I've achieved something, and I want you to treat me with the respect I've earned."

Can you pinpoint other turf where this creed might apply—perhaps *your office?* Challenges are won every day by the people who surround you.

Some of those wins are hole-in-one kind of efforts. Imagine their disappointment when no one cheers from the gallery. Is it any wonder employees often develop a nobody-really-cares-what-I-do kind of apathy?

Higher . . . faster . . . farther! Isn't that your goal—on and off the course? As a leader, you have witnessed enough PAR-formance from your staff. That's why you're reading this book. What you *really* want is PRO-formance! How can you make that happen? Your praise and recognition will provide the performance edge to transform your team players into champions.

While golf is not a game of brute strength, it *is* a contact sport. It all comes down to one fleeting millisecond . . . the point of contact between club and ball. That's the crucial instant when everything is determined.

Unfortunately, in business—as in golf—it's often the poor players who get the most strokes. Can we realize the importance of the point of contact—human contact and approval for *all* our players? That's the instant when everything is determined—motivation, attitude, and behavior.

Can you succeed without all the fuss of praising? Maybe. But who can take that chance? Mastering the art of great leadership—without the power of praise—depends on far too many "ifs" and "putts."

As a busy manager, you've got places to be other than standing guard over employee shoulders forty hours a week. No one is suggesting that.

When you *are* there, however, really be there for

your people. Remember, successful leadership is a game of contact—human contact. Don't be a manager-in-absentia who just putters around. Make the most of your presence—and theirs—by recognizing all the good you observe.

In the game of golf, or business, or life, each of us is part-time player, part-time spectator. Each morning marks the start of "the tournament." There are no practice rounds or driving ranges. When it's your turn, make it your best shot ever. When it's not your turn, be the most enthusiastic, spirited fan in the gallery! Every day. Every time. Every tee.

All of this high-flying talk leads us to one very down-to-earth conclusion: *Be there* to witness and applaud your staff's achievements *as they happen* and award with deserving recognition. It's the style of the masters. Try it. All you have to lose is your handicap.

"That's What He Gets
Paid the Big Bucks For!"

"But what about *my* manager who never compliments anything I do?"

The problem has already crossed your mind while reading this book.

Good question. Now here's a better one: When was the last time *you* praised *your* supervisor?

"But that's what he gets paid the big bucks for!" you protest. "If I were making his salary, I wouldn't need other perks to keep me going."

Really?

Just the thought of "boss praising" is a pretty weird idea for most of us. We assume our managers are getting *all the compensation they need monetarily.* If their responsibilities are demanding, then aren't they well paid for their trouble?

Does your manager want applause? Visualize your own reaction when one of *your* staff members praises you.

Believe it or not, managers are people, too. What we want is what they want, remember? Praising, or even criticizing your manager, indicates that you do pay attention to his actions and you care about the way you are supervised. Before you discount "boss praising" as baloney, at least consider this: it *is* possible to conduct yourself in such a way that your coworkers aren't constantly asking how you plan to wipe your nose . . . the drool off your chin.

This book is not endorsing BNTBG (brown-nosing the big guy). Or BLTBC (boot-licking the big cheese). Or APTTB (apple-polishing the top banana). Granted, enough kiss-up artistry is going on at this very moment to nauseate all of us. So, unless you want the reputation of a GATOMOSSU (guy/gal around the office most often seen schmoozing up), steer clear of those dubious activities. Offering *sincere* boss praise isn't easy. Chances are, you're breaking new ground. Still, your comments should follow the guidelines provided for giving recognition to your own staff: Be sincere. Be specific. Be brief. Be outta there.

Try it on your manager and expect a pleasant surprise. He's not accustomed to getting praise from down the line—nor perhaps from up the line, either!

Be contagious! Start a praise epidemic with your boss.

Follow up the unique idea of boss praise with yet another bold move. Give your supervisor a copy of this book. Tell her how it helped improve relationships with your staff. What better way to ignite the praise idea in her management style!

This stuff is contagious! A little "boss praise" plus this book and—who knows? Your boss may come down with a real case of HICGUTTS ("Hey, I could get used to this stuff!") You may start an epidemic.

But you must be infected before you can spread it. Your unexpected gift of praise will be a welcome bonus on top of all those "big bucks" he's already making!

"Mr. Sam" and
the Wall Street Hula

At age twenty-two, he cut his retailing teeth as a seventy-five-dollar-a-month trainee at J.C. Penney. Then he became the proud franchise owner of a Ben Franklin five-and-dime store. But he had bigger ideas. *Much* bigger. Moving his wife and four children into a rented house in a small Arkansas town, he opened his own store. He nailed an orange crate to the wall for use as a bookshelf. With two sawhorses and a sheet of plywood, he crafted a makeshift desk.

But thirty years later, Sam Walton and his namesake Wal-Mart stores surpassed Sears and KMart to become the nation's top retailer. His empire now stretches across the United States and employs nearly half a million associates. In the process, he became the wealthiest man in America.

How did he do it? Certainly not the conventional way. Known as "Mr. Sam" to his beloved employees, Walton defied traditional wisdom as he rewrote the rules of retailing and mass merchandising with a careful blend of business savvy, incredible energy, and a common touch that set him apart as an American original. A charismatic man, Mr. Sam was known to wear moderately priced suits, casual shoes, and an ever-present Wal-Mart baseball cap while tooling around town in his worn red and white pickup. At the time of his death in April 1992, Sam had amassed a personal family fortune of twenty-two billion dollars and nearly forty-four billion dollars in annual sales.

How could a man of such massive wealth live and work so unpretentiously? Sam's simple stay-in-touch-with-your-people style is one of the secrets of his success.

In 1983, Walton challenged his officers to produce a pre-tax profit of 8 percent for the coming year. If they succeeded, he promised to celebrate by dancing the hula on Wall Street. Much to the delight of Chairman Walton, Wal-Mart employees awarded their beloved founder his projected profit margin—and then some! Much to the delight of his employees, Mr. Sam kept his promise. Accompanied by a band of Hawaiian dancers and musicians, he slipped into a grass skirt and jiggled away!

How many corporate-collared stuffed shirts do *you* know who would publicly dance the Wall Street hula? Yet that's one major factor that made Sam Walton unique—and successful, *very* successful. It's just possible we can keep our pinstripes and power ties and still learn plenty from Mr. Sam's folksy style. International corporations frequently dispatch their key executives to Bentonville, Arkansas, to study the founder's business philosophy.

When a group of workers spends forty hours a week together, it's important that they like and respect each other. Sam's informal atmosphere fostered an environment in which his employees still thrive. The loyalty among Wal-Mart's employees is inspired by Sam's philosophy in which ideas and profits are shared freely. Sam learned the value of not taking himself too seriously, while showing his people that he was not too good to work alongside them in the store.

Walton's warm, humble manner welded an enormously strong connection among his staff. All store employees, from the lowest to the highest, are granted the title "associate."

"Once we started experimenting with this idea of treating our associates as partners, it didn't take long to realize the enormous potential it had for improving our business," Sam explained. Summarizing his winning relationship with his associate-partners, he termed it the "single smartest move we ever made."

Workers need a sense of pulling together—of being a team. Sam provided that with his common touch, his unassuming style, and his refusal to isolate himself from his people.

Walton conducted frequent store visits like pep rallies, leading the troops in a rousing corporate cheer: "Gimme a W! Gimme an A! Gimme an L!" In Memphis, he sat on the floor with staffers and listened to their ideas on how to stay ahead of the competition. In Winder, Georgia, Sam treated eight hourly employees to pizza to get their input for a new store.

"He is a master at erasing that larger-than-life feeling that people have for him," observed Andy Sims, store manager. "How many heads of state always start the conversation by wanting to know what *you* think? What's on *your* mind?"

While the recession prompted many businesses to eliminate all their perks, from stock ownership to coffee in the break room, Wal-Mart posted healthy revenue gains throughout stormy economic times.

Why? Sam Walton understood that there were factors just as important as beefing up ailing bottom lines by expense management. Walton realized his bottom line depended equally on the art of *people* management.

"You have to talk to the people," Walton disclosed. "You have to listen to them, mostly. You have to make them know that this is a *partnership*. That's our secret."

While many corporate leaders feel strongly about maintaining a professional distance from their work force, such philosophy never registered with Mr. Sam. That same "professional distance" often isolates the leader from reading the vital signs of his staff and operation.

Nowhere does the line "dance with the one who brung you" apply more aptly than here. Whatever success you achieve will be largely because of the dedicated efforts of those who work with you. Simple gestures such as rolling up your sleeves and pitching in to help with manual or mundane tasks will amplify team spirit. Staffers will recognize and appreciate that although you are the leader, you're a team member *first* and you don't flaunt a superior attitude. No other demonstration will produce greater loyalty among your staff!

So don your grass skirt and discover the perfect fit for improving morale and productivity among your staff. Pick your partner—your people! Stay close to them. Don't take yourself too seriously. Lighten up. Create fun and camaraderie. Share a laugh, a joke, a lighter moment at your own expense. Allow them to see *and* feel the human side of you.

Come on! They're playing your song! Put your best foot forward and get in step to humanize corporate leadership.

It had been *some* enchanted evening! One that spanned more than thirty years across a crowded room of corporate competitors. Upon being awarded the Presidential Medal of Freedom only days before his death, Mr. Sam lovingly deferred his lifelong success to his "partner," the same one he had chosen for the duration of his merchandising career—his people.

Make your people your partner. Allow them to see and feel the human side of you.

"This is a labor of partnership," explained Sam. "A labor of folks who have pulled together and have enjoyed what they've done and have become partners in what we've accomplished."

Hear it? It's beginning to sound like a familiar tune from the repertoire of phenomenal leaders everywhere.

Play it again, Sam!

You Have the Right
to Remain Silent

Brian, sales manager of a small advertising firm, stepped out of his office and sounded the siren he had installed in the storage closet. Suddenly everyone came running, applauding wildly.

What was all the fuss? Gerrie, a sales rep, had just signed a big account—one she'd been working on for months.

With the fervor of an evangelist, Brian briefed the staff on Gerrie's accomplishment and led a wild round of applause. He served ice cream cones. Fifteen minutes later, everyone went back to work.

Could you work for a company that expresses its gratitude in such a dramatic, fun way? Silly question.

Better question: Why don't *more* companies voice their gratitude to deserving employees in dramatic, fun ways?

The general consensus of modern management often implies, "Our deal is: you work, we pay. 'Thank you' is not part of the contract." In the workplace, the two most difficult words to pronounce are *Thank you!* It's a phrase that frequently dies in our throats.

Unfortunately, nobody wins in such an arrangement. Adequate recognition and appreciation will never be represented by a payroll check. The take-home pay is merely an exchange for prescribed duties. Earnings should be appreciated, but they do not represent a show of thanks on behalf of the company. Sincere gratitude must be demonstrated in ways that exhibit deliberate effort by leadership.

Administration that fails to show timely appreciation is squandering some real motivational opportunities. Voicing your praise and gratitude in a specific way is far too important to be left to chance.

Thank you! Thank you! Thank you! These two hard-to-pronounce syllables are forever on the top leader's tongue. They are the primer for mastering fluency in the language of "employee-ese." Recall how many times you could have uttered this two-syllable phrase. This no-cost reward inspires extra effort. If it works one time out of ten, your return on the investment will be worthwhile. Those in pursuit of a higher standard of leading are aware that people respond positively to appreciation and applause—even when they insist otherwise.

Make "thank you" a part of your working vocabulary.

"You have the right to remain silent," they tell us. What an arresting notion! Freedom of speech is our constitutional right.

"Anything you say can be used against you . . ." Sure, it might happen. That's the very reason many managers remain mute. Praise leaves them vulnerable. What if their display of gratitude backfires? Is that a valid reason *not* to use a tool that has proven so successful?

No.

Yes, you *do* have the right to remain silent. You

also have the right to remain marginal, mundane and mediocre. The lesson is elementary. Reap surprising benefits from a simple expression of gratitude. Those two seldom pronounced words can inspire results that belie their simplicity. Anything you say (in the way of gratitude) can and will be attributed to your leadership success.

It's not necessary to concern yourself with proper form when saying thank you. Nowhere else does "do what comes naturally" fit more suitably than here. When you express thanks, look your recipient in the eye, smile, shake hands if you wish, and offer your thank-yous warmly. Most of us don't say them often enough. Successful leaders do.

Now you've got the basics with a pair of simple vocabulary words. You're on your way to fluency in the language of "employee-ese!"

Watch Out for Those Reds!

After accepting a performance review from his manager, Clay went over the written feedback form meticulously with highlighter pens. He accented the negative comments in red and the positive ones in blue.

Clay then returned and asked Sybil, his manager, to summarize how she *really* felt about his overall performance.

"Actually, I'm quite pleased with your work, Clay," Sybil replied.

He then showed her his copy of the appraisal form, colored appropriately with positive and negative distinctions.

"I was staring at a sea of red with a sporadic blue line drawn here and there," confessed Sybil. "That kind of evidence really made me realize how negative I had been, even though I was mostly pleased."

Annual performance reviews provide a platform for offering applause to your team members, and this is the *only* time many workers get specific feedback. As in Clay's case, annual reviews often result in traumatic and emotional confrontations that may threaten an employee's sense of security.

Remember when you were in school and the teacher returned test papers? Even though you scored a passing grade, the page was bleeding profusely. The blood-red scrawl across your page seemed to scream, *How dumb of you to get these wrong!*

Barbara Gurley, teacher at the Gib Lewis prison

unit in Huntsville, Texas, has perfected the art of positive feedback. As a Reading Specialist, Mrs. Gurley is keenly aware that her students have met failure and frustration throughout most of their school years.

"I find marking the *right* answers—not the wrong ones—gives students a sense of doing something right," Mrs. Gurley wrote me. "We build on that!"

The same technique works equally well in the business arena. A few years ago, Preston Trucking, a Maryland-based carrier, suffered unhealthy management-labor relations. After a lengthy standoff, top management resolved to treat the problem by implementing numerous innovative reforms. One new technique was the "Four-to-One" rule: For every criticism a manager made about a driver's performance, he had to offer him four positive comments.

Occasionally, every manager's agenda involves targeting areas for improvement. Regrettably, many managers excel here while failing to focus on the positive. We must be willing to acknowledge the good as well as the not-so-good.

Have you noticed how many things we view from a negative point of view? Do you ever read a yard sign announcing *Nice Dog?* Rather than publishing birth announcements, newspapers feature obituaries. Instead of a 70 percent chance of sunshine, it's a 30 percent chance of rain! While the news media keeps us up-to-date on international conflicts, only *one percent* of the world's population is actually involved in war.

Why is it that we can perform our duties almost

perfectly and no one seems to notice? When you're right, it seems no one remembers. When you're wrong, it seems no one forgets. Make one small error, and . . . "gotcha!" The manager instantly springs into action to arrest his violating employee. Such practice is immature and produces a negative reaction that undermines the relationship.

Coauthor of *The One-Minute Manager,* Ken Blanchard offers the cure for ailing managers addicted to the "gotcha" game. In most corporations, Blanchard insists, managers spend most of their time catching people doing something wrong. Adopt Blanchard's technique of catching your employee in "the act of doing something *right.*"

Pinpoint and proclaim the positives in your people.

"Only a small portion of feedback should be critical," advises Robert C. Dorn, director of training at the Center for Creative Leadership in Greensboro, North Carolina. "People should be doing things right about 80 percent of the time, so most feedback should be positive. Twenty percent or less should be negative."

Too many managers are keeping score and the ratio is negatively stacked. In this intense match of "pokes versus strokes," the score should be at least four to one in favor of the strokes. Adjust your game plan accordingly.

When offering written feedback, learn from Sybil's mistake and from Barbara's experience to ensure that the "reds" don't take over. Why not use highlighter pens to accent exemplary employee performance? When the review is conducted, the employee's attention will be immediately drawn to the positive aspects of their performance rather than the negative.

If most of our job is done correctly, wouldn't it be nice to have someone recognize *that* fact in addition to the areas needing improvement?

Remember, if the "reds" win, *everybody* loses!

Pink Trophy on Wheels
and Other Gold Stars

Diamond rings! Necklaces! Bracelets! Mink coats! European and Hawaiian vacations! Giveaway Buicks and Cadillacs! Is it a publicity contest or a sweepstakes promotion?

No and yes.

No, it's not the typical commercial gimmick to lure you into a magazine subscription you didn't want. And yes, it *does* make all the employees at Mary Kay Cosmetics feel like sweepstakes champions. But Mary Kay's winners are not selected through games of chance.

The most prominent name in the cosmetics industry, Mary Kay Ash, reveals the prime secret of her success in *Contemporary Authors*. "Because we recognize the need for people to be praised, we make a concentrated effort to give as much recognition as possible . . . when a Mary Kay consultant drives a pink Cadillac, it really is a trophy on wheels, and she is recognized as a person who has done an outstanding job. It signifies that she is very important in our organization. And, of course, once she achieves this important status, she doesn't ever want to relinquish the privilege."

Dazzling prizes are the conspicuous components of Mary Kay's dramatic, glamorous style. But she gives much more! Thousands of ribbons costing only a few cents are presented to deserving beauty consultants and directors. Mary Kay ushers them on stage to revel in there-she-is-Miss-America kind of applause. In addition, she publishes three separate magazines to document and applaud in print her top achievers.

Mary Kay has learned, practiced, and perfected the gold star creed. She terms this "praising people to success." Her strongest form of applause costs nothing at all. It is simply praise.

"I believe that you should praise people whenever you can; it causes them to respond as a thirsty plant responds to water," advises Mary Kay (*Mary Kay on People Management,* Warner, 1984).

Successful organizations who value sincere recognition allocate funds for specifically saying thanks. Of course, you don't gift everyone lavishly just because he's doing his job. And not all companies can afford to give away expensive trophies.

Embellish your praise with frequent gold stars.

Be quick to reward extraordinary performance by whatever means you can. A pair of tickets to a sports event or the theater, dinner, or a day off with pay announces to everyone on your team that you recognize exceptional performance. Or enter your employee's work in industry competition. Or nominate him for an award. Or allow him to attend a seminar or self-improvement workshop at company expense.

"Get real!" skeptics protest. "That sounds like kiddie stuff—like the gold stars plastered at the top of our paper when we did good work."

Exactly. The same principle applies here—and produces the same warm feelings experienced by the grade-schooler. Grown-ups like gold stars too—maybe more than the kids!

In his best seller *All You Can Do Is All You Can Do,* insurance magnate A. L. Williams features a gold-star idea. During the early years, Williams found himself lacking the cash needed to buy plaques for his top sales staff. "One day it came to me," Williams recalls. "I would give T-shirt awards, just like I had given to the high school football players when I was coaching. I presented those 'awards,' and the people loved them. The slogans were simple, and some were funny. Today, over ten years and a lot of success later, I give lots of different awards. But the T-shirt awards are still the most popular—and the most fun."

Think about it. How much recognition does the average worker receive during his life? Maybe a couple of little league trophies, a high school diploma, a twenty-year service pin—and not much else.

So what should that mean to *you?*

Wake up! Here's your chance to break new ground for hungry acceptance of your praise—favor that will likely yield huge returns from your freshly committed employee. There's plenty of room for finding creative new ways to reward a job well done.

"When you work with people," explained Andrew Carnegie, "it is a lot like mining for gold . . . you must literally move tons of dirt to find a single ounce of gold . . . you do not look for the dirt—you look for the gold!"

In whatever ways you find the gold in others, you will be richer for rewarding it with your own golden response. Practice new awareness of the good that happens around you for creating more gold-star moments!

If we are to succeed, we must learn from, appreciate, and reward our employees. And, as Mary Kay discovered, once employees enjoy that gold-star status, they'll do their best to keep it! The gold stars are important to them, and they are *essential* for us in our pursuit of a higher standard of leading.

Just *how* high do you want to go?

"What Does It Take to Get a Little Appreciation Around This Place?"

Executive secretary Michelle never heard from her boss, David, unless the quality of her work was below par. Then he was hasty to point out the defects. Although Michelle knew she did a good job, often a superior job, David never voiced his approval. Michelle didn't really want a continual gush of applause, but she did reasonably expect occasional acknowledgement.

"After all," she fumed, "just what does it take to get a little appreciation around this place?"

Simply telling Michelle her work was appreciated would have made the difference between productivity and resentment. In the process, David would have reinforced the norms he expected—hard work and dedication.

Are you one of those faithful managers who remembers his secretary on Professional Secretary's Day? Could you be one of those unfaithful managers, like David, who ignores his secretary every other day of the calendar year?

People who need praise most are the ones most often overlooked. Most professionals enjoy intrinsic benefits in their duties that provide satisfaction. Grand recognition is often presented at the conclusion of a successful project. Players on the winning team are honored with awards, bonuses, and various other perks.

But what about those positions in which success isn't as apparent? Workers who play supporting roles

are often overlooked in favor of the more visible employees. We often exert the loudest applause for the
obvious wins, yet we are surrounded every day by
obscure individual victories.

Would our goals and projects be possible without
the contribution of these people? Never! They strive
just as hard and achieve just as much. But because
their vital functions are not visible, they are often
ignored.

Credit your
vital-but-not-visible
support staff.

In her book *Good Bosses Do,* Betsy Lazary explains
that recognition doesn't have to mean banquets,
speeches, and grand honors. "Going overboard with
good intentions can backfire because professional sec-
retaries react negatively to patronizing. Recognition
should occur on a regular basis, not just during an
annual review or on Professional Secretary's Day."

Adapt these small but important courtesies for
making your support staff feel appreciated:

- Introduce your support staff to clients and associates. Create a feeling of importance.
- Write positive notes on the paperwork your secretary or staff will see. Note pads featuring "way-to-
  go" messages generate positive feelings.
- Personally inform your assistants of the end result
  of office projects. If your support crew has been

right in there with you on a long, challenging project, inform them firsthand of its success. Include them in project wrap-up meetings, post-parties, and celebrations.

- Publicly acknowledge your staff's contribution on a project. Let everyone see you are secure enough to share the glory with all parties responsible.

- "We couldn't have done it without you!" Adopt this attitude as part of your working vocabulary. You can't lose if you say it sincerely. The feeling of being indispensable is a glowing reward for your team.

- Make an effort to inform everyone, including upper management, of your total team effort. Write a memo detailing their roles in your project. Send it to your boss. And his boss. And his boss! No one will be offended by such consideration. Print is cheap, but the rewards are priceless.

Think about the last movie you saw. Can you name the leading roles? Probably. Can you name any of the editors, stuntmen, or technicians? Probably not.

In every Hollywood movie production, hundreds of staff assistants, editors, extras, stuntmen, and technical crews work behind the scenes. We would hardly know they exist except for the endless roll of credits stashed on the end of the reel. Only a handful of actors grab the recognition, exposure, and attention of the viewers. But no movie would *ever* be finished without the total team effort of the supporting cast.

Most often, *you* are the star of your production. In business, there's no such thing as a one-man show. Remember those numerous supporting roles, the nameless crew members working in the file rooms, mail rooms, copy rooms, and warehouses of your "studio." Their contributions are essential to your program. Include them in your "credits." They're the ones who make your show go on and on.

Whether your production is grossing millions at the box office or a mere paycheck on the first of the month, your manners should be the same. Surprising benefits will blossom around you. And your people will thrive under the spotlight of your praise.

"No matter what your business or career is, you can't do it alone," advises A. L. Williams in *All You Can Do Is All You Can Do*. "The more success you have, the more likely it is that you will have other people on your 'success team.' How you treat those people can make the difference in whether your business takes off or falls flat."

So what does it take to get a little appreciation around this place? One dedicated manager who feels secure enough to share the spotlight with everyone responsible for his success!

The 10-Point Checklist No Manager Should Be Caught Without!

Senior Vice President Mr. I. M. Boss suddenly appears in front of your desk.

"How is your team doing?" he wants to know.

You mumble something between a yawn and okay.

More specifically, he probes, "How do you rate the performance of your staff? You want to tell me about it?"

What is your answer?

(a) "I don't have any complaints."

(b) "They're doing fine."

(c) "They get the job done."

(d) "I've got a pretty good bunch here."

If your appraisal echoes these lines, you've got company. You're also in need of clearer, more specific focus. Nothing in these responses hints anything more than average job performance, nor does it indicate that you have bothered to notice.

Do you really *know* your employee? How well? What have you done with this information? What specific actions could you *now* take to empower your employee while reaping greater effort and increased productivity?

Maybe you haven't given it much thought. You should! Review the questions on the checklist to define your present skills as a positive motivator and productive leader.

To be totally effective, complete the checklist for every person you manage. Make it your priority to review and update the checklist regularly. Set a goal to discover and tell each of your employees what he has contributed this week and how much you appreciate his efforts.

You are sitting on a gold mine of productivity. Implement this checklist and tap in to a vein of pure gold. It's imperative to frequently study and know your people, not only to motivate them but to maximize your available human resources.

The match between the employee and his job cannot be overemphasized. You must make a conscious, continual effort to create the proper kind of challenge for your worker. When an employee perceives that his talents and skills are not being recognized and utilized, job dissatisfaction sets in quickly. Unless conditions change, he soon looks elsewhere for more challenging career opportunities.

Look for the best *in* them to get the best *out* of them!

A New Jersey computer firm recently polled one hundred professionals who had left their company to determine specific reasons for leaving. Management was surprised to discover that 25 percent cited "lack of opportunity to use ability."

How much more beneficial it will be for you to implement ideas and programs to keep workers motivated and challenged. Or you can watch them walk away and then ask, "What went wrong?"

When a position begins to feel terminal, mechanical or ho-hum, jumpstart your staffers by shifting job responsibilities. Cross-pollinate! Provide opportunities for learning new job functions.

Or invite their input directly: "What responsibilities are you currently *not* doing here that you *would* like to do?" It could be you'll uncover hidden talents, dynamic ideas, and fresh motivation that will serve your purposes better than ever. But you'll never know unless you're willing to be flexible and experiment with your resources.

"If you want to get the best *out* of a man," declares Bernard Haldane, "you must look for the best *in* him." *Read* his maximum potential to *reap* his maximum performance!

Begin your checklist to experience phenomenal results. No manager should be caught without it!

And the next time Mr. Senior V.P. comes strolling through unannounced, you'll be ready!

10-Point Checklist

Employee name: _____

Date of hire: _____ / _____ / _____

✔ How well do I know this person? What facts or details can I readily recall about his/her family, personal goals, and outside interests? _____
_____

✔ What do I know specifically about his/her career plans—both short-term and long-term goals? _____
_____

✔ What one word or phrase best describes his/her job performance? _____

✔ If he/she resigned today, what would I miss most?
_____

✔ What is his/her greatest strength, contribution, talent, or specialty? _____
_____

✔ When was the last time I discussed the potential of this strength or talent directly with him/her? _____
_____

✔ What have I done recently to make him/her feel an important part of my staff? _____
_____

✔ When was the last time I sat down with him/her and asked for his/her input, ideas, or job preferences?
_____

✔ What specific, positive comment can I offer him/her *today* regarding his/her strength, talent, or contribution? _____

✔ Based on my responses here, what one new idea can I implement *now* to maximize his/her specialty or talent within my organization? _____
_____

Figure 2

Can I Be a Manager and a Person, Too?

Is it possible to utilize your PraisePower and maintain integrity and respect as a professional?

Yes! Consider the issues discussed here to alter your style accordingly.

Watch out! The results will be astounding as you begin to support your people through verbal applause.

Can I Praise Too Much?

Yes. If recognition comes too frequently, it loses its impact. Too much of a good thing diminishes its effectiveness.

Excessive praise can establish a pattern you prefer not to continue. And it may give employees the impression you expect a flawless job every time.

Should I Praise All Employees Equally?

Do all employees perform equally? No. Do all employees exert the same amount of effort? No. Then your praise should be commensurate with their performance or efforts.

Consistent workers require less reinforcement than those striving to improve. Praising the same desirable behavior repeatedly may become ineffective, but those learning new responsibilities need continual, attentive feedback until their skills become routine.

Is Timing Really Important?

Recognition should follow the well-executed act as quickly as possible to clarify and focus the object of your praise. Your employee's accomplishment is fresh on his mind for only a short time. Voicing immediate approval assures that the performance will be duplicated. Your employee understands exactly what is being praised—and what should be repeated.

If a laudable action occurs today, voice your appreciation today. Delaying verbal reaction until sometime after the fact often communicates a by-the-way attitude that diminishes the effect. Dramatize your praise for maximum effect by springing to action as you "catch" the employee in the praiseworthy act.

Should Praise Be Public or Private?

A busy insurance executive uses weekly team meetings as a platform for expressing his appreciation to praiseworthy staffers. As a result, he is surrounded by fiercely loyal and productive people who are motivated by his praise.

Appraise your applause.

Let your applause be heard by more than just the recipient. An audience magnifies the significance and validates worth among the group that workers are most concerned about—their peers. And your listeners often get as charged as your champion. Guess who will exert extra effort to earn their reward next time?

Corky Epperson, training manager for Federal Express Corporation, wields a powerful tool for praising the individual accomplishments of his staff. Since his team is scattered throughout major cities of the Southeast, frequent staff meetings are not feasible. Instead, he writes a note of appreciation to the deserving employee with immediate distribution to the entire staff—and upper management—via electronic mail. Imagine how good *that* feels—having your peers (as well as your superiors) read your praise mail from the boss. There's no "high" like it!

"What gets rewarded, gets done!" he says convincingly. "And it ensures, in almost all cases, that excellent contributions will continue."

Epperson is wisely aware that praise does more than recognize a deserving employee. His applause announces to the entire crew that exceptional performance will be recognized *and* rewarded.

Can Praise Be Used for Corrective Measures?

Absolutely! If you consciously praise a worker for something you want him to do, the odds of him doing it increase considerably. Children and adults alike respond more readily to praise than to punishment.

A study of chronically late employees indicated that commending the infrequent prompt arrival proved more convincing than reprimanding the late employee.

Corrective measures? A wise manager will take care of the problem proactively, but not in a criticizing manner. If praise is effective, then the *absence* of praise is equally convincing. Just as employees will strive to warrant your consistent applause, they recognize when you suppress it.

How Can I Determine If My Praise Is Effective?

The key is perception. You may grade yourself high for exerting extraordinary efforts at praising your team, but they may perceive things quite differently.

Create your own evaluation survey to provide candid, confidential feedback on employee perceptions. Or conduct an open forum at your next staff meeting to stimulate ideas and healthy communication.

What If My Praise Sounds the Same Every Time?

Strive to keep your praise fresh, personalized, and specific. Avoid routine comments. Announcing "Great job, guys!" every other day isn't praise—it's habit.

Smile at your target. Look directly into his eyes. Call him *by name*. Tell him *exactly* what he did to win your approval: "Ben, your report on the Heinz project was right on the mark. It gave our client exactly what he needed, and he's ready to sign the contract."

PraisePower means understanding your people. When they do good work, they want their boss not only to know it but to recognize *in detail* how it was achieved. The boss who quips "good job!" provides a pinch of satisfaction, but how much more effective praise *could* be with a bit more energy invested!

Allow your employee the joy of explaining how she

accomplished her challenge. Ask questions you know your employee will enjoy answering. Watch her glow with the pride of her accomplishment as she explains specifically how she completed the task. Sharing ideas or information with the boss gives most people tremendous personal satisfaction.

And the best part? Your people will work harder to achieve similar or better results next time. Isn't that ample reward for appraising your own applause?

They get what *they* want and you get what *you* want. Now that's a deal that's almost "two" good to be true!

How to Stay Dry
Under the Shower of Praise

Him: "Hey, nice job on the Fischer account!"
You: a) "What can I say?"
     b) "Anyone could've done it."
     c) "It would've been better if only I . . ."
     d) "It was really nothing."

Though the major focus of this book underlines the need and the means for offering praise, *accepting* praise is often equally difficult.

Getting the good word can make you feel bad or at least a little self-conscious. Under the shower of praise, we often grow uncomfortable, almost mimicking the squirming, toe-digging reactions of a child.

Sociologists Charles Edgley and Ronny Turner eavesdropped on enough real-life conversations to find 245 of them that included compliments. Their subsequent interviews with the recipients were startling. While most recipients felt deserving, they experienced difficulty accepting praise. To appear modest, many subjects believed they had to deny full responsibility for the achievement. "Well, I can't take all the credit," they mutter, "I had a lot of help" (*Reader's Digest,* October, 1975).

Praise, the sweetest of all sounds, may make us uneasy—even queasy. Even though we want, need and regularly fish for compliments, once we land them we hardly know how to react. Here is an area where most of us fumble. Someone aims an admiring comment in our direction and we blush, we gush, and our mouth turns to mush.

If it's any comfort, praise has always had its consequences. In some cultures, if Person X admired something belonging to Person Y, Person Y had to *give* it to Person X. (Think about *that* next time someone admires your briefcase, your window office, or your secretary.)

Still other cultures practiced a creative exercise in which one compliment had to be returned with another, which would then have to be reciprocated . . . which in turn would be pretty exhausting by late afternoon!

Even in our culture, we feel we must return the compliment, just as we feel obliged to return a dinner invitation or a holiday card. We tend to feel it incumbent upon us to even the score promptly.

Learn to accept praise graciously.

Taught from early childhood not to blow our own horns, we can't seem to get used to other people blowing them for us. We fear we might imply arrogance. We easily express thanks for material gifts, but accepting the immaterial gift of praise is an undeveloped social skill. Yet refuting a compliment gives your praiser an awkward, deflated feeling as though you're refusing his thoughtful gift.

Accepting praise may also cause worry that we won't be able to maintain whatever virtue is being extolled. We may panic that "next time" we might not do as well.

Kind words may be resented if we feel we are being judged. The very act of giving praise implies that the praiser is, at least momentarily, sitting in judgment, and that is never a comfortable feeling. Finally, praise may often make us suspect the giver's true intent. Most of us have been corrected and criticized so much that we invariably analyze it first.

Perhaps the most important clue to enjoying a compliment lies in knowing how to respond to one.

Smile

If smiling is not a natural reaction for you, force yourself. A smile adds a great deal to your "face value." Concentrate on this physical act until it becomes a conditioned reflex. At the sound of a compliment, your smiling response is automatic—and sincere.

Accept with Thanks

Now, you are ready for verbal expression. Don't rush in to deny it, return it, or change the subject. Accept with graciousness. Not only will the praiser be happier, but it will also reveal your own self-confidence.

The only sensible response consists of eight letters arranged neatly into two small words: "Thank you."

Fight the Urge to Oblige

Resist the conditioned reflex to return every compliment you receive. Save it for another occasion when your comments will seem fresh and sincere.

Or flavor your thanks with a hint of appreciation by adding, "It's nice of you to mention it."

Enjoy!

After a brief thanks, inhale deeply to let the compliment flow through you like warm energy. Recognize your good qualities, the fact that someone else noticed, and . . . ahhh . . . enjoy!

Save Your Oilcan
and Rag for Later

At some point in this book, you have probably muttered: "Huh, this won't work for me," or "That would never fly around here!"

Your business is unique. However, people are all pretty much the same. Basic needs, drives, and responses vary little. *Human relations will work wherever there are humans!*

The challenge is to follow the ideas given here, together with the tools you have, modifying and improvising them wherever necessary to meet your objective.

Your first impression of this book may be that it's impractical, management-by-heart rhetoric claiming to cure all corporate ills: Treat your staff sweetly. Trust them blindly. Make sure everyone adores you.

That is *not* the objective of this book. What it offers is a distinct exodus from the management style we see in prevalent practice today.

There is an urgent need for nurturing a healthy respect and appreciation for our people. Leaders must view all of their workers as contributing, capable, and sensitive human beings rather than as production machines. The leader who has recognized the genuine worth of his employees can produce an atmosphere where phenomenal performance is possible *and* probable.

In spite of our supersonic generation, high-tech wizardry, and computer gadgetry, there is no technical tool equal to praise. As long as we are working with humans, PraisePower will be among our finest allies for assuring leadership success. When—if ever—workers are replaced with robots, then we can throw this book away and get ourselves an oilcan and a rag to maintain a smooth-running corporate machine!

This book challenges you to focus on the best in others. Every person possesses some extraordinary gift. Great leaders identify each employee's flair and talents, then nourish them to maximum use.

In this way, your staff members win by learning to accept their own self-worth. Your organization wins through increased profits and productivity. You win by getting the results you want from your team.

Finally, *practice* praising. A lot! There's a good chance you won't hear many complaints. It's not like you're honking a tuba or crooning "The Battle Hymn of the Republic" in the shower. No need to worry. Praise is generally welcome in ears weary from the clamor and noise of life.

You are looking for ways to fine-tune your skills or you would never have read this far. Successful leaders hunger incessantly for new ideas and better methods.

Accept the challenge. Adopt these concepts. Store your oilcan. Stuff the rag for later. Be exceptional. No, be *phenomenal* in your human relations!

You won't be too far out—just way out *front!*

THREE

Pursue a Higher Standard of Learning

◆

Nothing improves a child's
hearing like praise.

◆

Chapter Objectives

○ Remember, there's no time like the present; there's no present like your time.

○ Focus on the "I cans" and the "IQs" will take care of themselves.

○ Realize that, next to love, praise is the greatest gift we can give our children!

○ Play fair. Maintain an equal balance of throw-and-catch in all your family communications.

○ Reassure your child daily: "I love you no matter what happens."

○ Be alert to the rich life lessons your child will teach you.

○ Be an Impressionist! Apply frequent strokes to create a parent's masterpiece.

○ Do your homework! Target and review your child's strengths with him regularly.

○ Qualify your praise with specifics for maximum impact.

○ Recognize that the presence or absence of your encouragement may spell the difference between triumph and tragedy.

This book is for you, the caring parent and teacher. You are looking for the key to help your child succeed in his studies, social graces, physical development, and in life! Having met with hundreds of parents in parent-teacher conferences, I always find one factor is evident: I have never met a parent who wanted anything but the best for his child. Desire and good intentions were always present. What was frequently lacking was the knowledge and direction to nurture the child's success.

What can you do to be successful in parenting or teaching? Should you purchase the latest and greatest encyclopedias? How about a course in speed reading? Would a personal computer be the answer?

There is no hocus-pocus plan to guarantee success for your children, but there are several definite ways you can improve their chances.

You don't have to be a professional teacher to provide your child with a stimulating learning environment. You don't need a college degree. You need not be a psychologist. You already have the sole essential ingredient—or you wouldn't be reading this book. Your desire to improve your current skills will lead you to success.

No one can forecast the critical challenges your child will encounter. Yet you can gift him with the foundation necessary to meet each situation. The groundwork should not be left to chance. There is much you can do to improve the odds. Your personal involvement is never more critical than during these formative years. Now's the time to give it all you've got!

There's No Present
Like Your Time!

"Hey, watch me, Mommy! Daddy! Look at me!"

Many times a day, busy parents hear this cry and stop to notice: "Aren't you a good soldier! . . . a good baker! . . . a good builder!"

Or perhaps, engrossed in their chores, Mom and Dad don't answer. Then the persistent cry crescendos to a ceremonial war whoop—until the parent *does* respond.

The "watch me's" escalate as the child discovers new challenges, activities, and abilities.

The excited child with his "look-at-me" request conveys what each of us expresses—only he's too innocent to mask it! He openly asks someone to share the joy of his accomplishment!

While expressions of approval are vital at the beginning of a career, they are even more critical at the dawn of life. Children have yet to discover from life experience that time mends most tragedies, that bad happens along with good, and that failure is often followed by success.

While each of us requires praise, children need it most. A two- or three-week-old infant will focus on her mother's face for that approving, glowing expression. "A positive, smiling acceptance, the look that says 'I am lucky to have you' mirrors an infant's sense of self," states Dr. Bernice Berk, a New York psychologist, (*Redbook*, June 1984).

From birth to six years comprises the fastest term of growth in human development. At no other time will you exert greater influence on your child. Almost all of her later experiences will hinge on what happens now.

No one is better equipped for teaching a child in her first six years than you—her parent. You have an immeasurable investment in her future. Providing a maximum start requires no special training or expense. You must be your child's first, best teacher!

> Remember, there's no time
> like the present; there's no
> present like your time.

Whether or not you will be the best teacher depends on what preparation you're willing to make. You have the desire. Coupled with direction, you're on your way.

We can give our children too much of everything, except ourselves. For launching your child on the route to positive attitudes, there's no time like the present. For gifting him with the best quality advantage, there's no present like your time!

"I Can!" or IQ?

"When Jarett came to my third grade class, he had given up," wrote JoAnn Williams, a teacher in Utica, New York.

Her letter to me continued, "He could read only a few words. My constant encouragement and praise followed every attempt he made. Patience paid off as Jarett's academic progress turned around. In one school term, he advanced three years in reading level! Suddenly, he started to like himself, and his self-image began to grow. Praise works miracles!" she enthused with intensity.

Mrs. Williams' contagious joy of learning infects the attitudes her students exhibit on both sides of the classroom door. "I've seen students from troubled backgrounds blossom and flourish in praise-filled classrooms. Jarett's attitude toward learning will be enhanced by the new beliefs he has about himself."

Self-esteem is a part of your child's development that cannot be left to chance. Much like a video camera, your child is absorbing every life experience to assess his own worth. Children who feel loved, respected, and encouraged generally enjoy higher self-worth.

Success in school is directly linked to students' self-esteem. A student with high IQ but a low self-image may perform poorly, and children with average abilities and high self-esteem are more likely to excel.

A study by Wattenberg and Clifford examined kindergarten children to determine the effects of high self-concept in comparison to high IQ. Amazingly, higher IQ children with low self-image did not learn to read as soon or as well as their classmates with higher self-esteem (*100 Ways to Enhance Self-Concept in the Classroom,* Prentice Hall, *1976*).

A good self-concept is equally important outside the classroom. Critical decisions made during the school-age years are influenced by a child's sense of self-worth. Decisions whether or not to use drugs, drop out of school, or become sexually active are influenced by self-image.

> Focus on the "I cans" and
> the "IQs" will take care
> of themselves.

What can you do to ensure your child has a positive self-image? You can easily raise your child's "I can" quotient by focusing on the positive. The result of criticizing our children is often an "I can't" quotient, lowering their self-esteem. "I can't" leads to feelings of inadequacy and failure.

"As a child, I have no recollection of a teacher ever saying anything positive to me in a classroom," recalls Louise Mears, a retired New York school teacher. "It was just a job for them. Their lack of praise brought on a lack of self-esteem I suffered for years. Building self-worth is the most important accomplishment we can make in a child," Mears advises.

Become more aware of all the "I cans" your child

accomplishes. Take photographs. Tell the grandparents and the neighbors. Offer credit publicly when you can without embarrassing the child. Teenagers may shrink from praise in the presence of peers but relish hearing one adult tell another about their praiseworthy act. Watch how "I cans" at home translate into "I cans" at school.

Recalling his days as a high school teacher, Atlanta corporate trainer Bill Wallace emphasizes the importance of creating an "I can" attitude.

I was teaching American history for mostly college-bound students. In my class was Jon, a senior who had failed the course the year before. A marginal student at best, he needed my course just to graduate.

Realizing Jon's limitations, I offered alternatives to the usual, required fifteen-page research paper. Continual encouragement and recognition paid off for both of us. My marginal 'problem student' produced an oil painting depicting a collage of events in historical sequence. Fueled with newfound confidence in his ability, Jon made a brilliant presentation to the class, describing the illustrated events. I was so impressed I bought Jon's painting, and it hangs in my home today.

Jon is a lucky guy to have enjoyed Wallace as his teacher. Other marginal students are not so fortunate. Imagine the failure, disappointment, and lower self-esteem Jon might have suffered in many classrooms.

Remember *your* favorite teacher from school?

What made him a favorite? Chances are good he somehow communicated a sense of caring, enhancing your own personal worth.

Can you recall your worst teacher? What made him the worst? Humiliation? Sarcasm? Ridicule? All of these foster a negative self-image lingering long after graduation.

Rick Alvarado, a San Antonio, Texas elementary school principal, illustrates the beauty of the "I can" theory in action:

> While observing in a classroom, the teacher asked students to read simple sentences from a placard. Calling on Alex, a low achiever, the teacher held up the card. Alex looked at it and said: 'I can't read.'
>
> The teacher replied, 'Sure you can, I will help you!' With help from the teacher, Alex read the sentence haltingly. As I left the classroom, I wrote Alex a note telling him how much I enjoyed listening to him read.
>
> A week later, Alex came to my office and read a short story to me. He is well on his way, thanks to a caring teacher who focused on what Alex *could* do and not on what he couldn't do. The key to reaching people is to focus on their strengths and to build upon them. Everyone has something to offer, and it is our responsibility as educators to make people aware that their contributions are important (taken from a letter to the author).

Principal Alvarado supports this theorem for successful learning: Nurture a positive self-image by focusing on the "*I cans*," and the *IQs* will take care of themselves!

Is It Just a
Praise-Phrase-Craze?

"Won't our praise-bathed children be ill-prepared for the cold, cruel world?"

"Is such positive awareness realistic?"

"Isn't this just a 'psychological piece of candy'?"

"Won't too much of this stuff lead to praise-addicted adults in constant need of an ego fix?"

Occasionally, a professional will surface and question this business of praise as being just another trendy fad we should outgrow. "Won't patterns of verbal applause make our children constantly dependent on the opinions and approval of others?" they ask.

Could be. However, before you reject this book as part of a praise-phrase-craze, check out the facts. In a 1992 *Newsweek* poll, the Gallup organization revealed that *89 percent of Americans believe self-esteem plays a major role* in motivating us to work harder and achieve success.

Do you think time spent praising others and nurturing self-esteem *is* worthwhile? At least 63 percent of us agree, according to the same Gallup findings. Overwhelming evidence shows that praise brings positive results in *all* areas of human relations—at home, in the classroom, on the ball field, and in the workplace. If you have the slightest interest in improving *any* of these areas, keep reading.

At their innocent birth, at the tender age of four, at the susceptible age of six, at the precarious age of thirteen, your children are seeking approval. Perhaps they don't deserve approval, you protest, and you wouldn't impair them by being oblivious to their defects and mistakes. You have no intent of coddling them now, just to make their grown-up experience more perplexing.

Well-intentioned as we might be, it's often difficult for us to realize that our offspring are wonderful when we often don't feel that way about ourselves. As products of a put-down society we have come to believe that it is a vice to be confident or self-assured. As a result, we often fail to provide children with the comforting support without which they feel vulnerable and insecure.

Realize that, next to love, praise is the greatest gift we can give our children!

"When parents come to me with their child's behavior problem," explains Dr. Barry Lubetkin in an article in *Redbook*, "I ask them if they regularly praise themselves and each other. Then I ask them how many times a day they praise their child. Often they're surprised at how infrequently they do. So we start there; we increase the praise."

Unfortunately, the pattern of low self-esteem perpetuates itself for generations until someone breaks the cycle. Voicing approval of your children is a prime method for experiencing positive change. The most valuable gift you can give your family is a good example.

The ego is never so stable that we can't uncover a crack in which to plug a bit of appreciation. But compliments are largely biodegradable and can wither very soon, which is why we can make good use of another . . . and another.

In his book *Psychology for Business and Industry,* Herbert Moore reports scientific studies which indicate praise is more than a craze. Out of 200 persons involved in one case study, *only one* reacted to praise negatively, while 87.5 percent actually improved their work quality.

Dr. Ben Williams, a Houston psychologist, validates verbal applause in a letter to me. Having witnessed the effects of praise-starved patients, Dr. Williams explains, "Children grow up in dislocated fashion and perceive their world inaccurately without praise, reward, and emotional satisfaction. Praise, or its absence, is the major means of teaching—emotionally, socially, and academically. Praise is basic to our existence and to our positive enjoyment of others and self."

World famous heart surgeon Dr. Denton Cooley assesses the benefits of praise from his perspective. "In the quest for healthier hearts, we cannot afford to discount either the power of the emotions or the potential of the healing word," Dr. Cooley explains. "Praise is the easiest and least expensive way to compensate one's employees, friends, and loved ones; to keep morale high; and to further interpersonal harmony."

Entertainer Pat Boone echoes similar sentiments.

"If God Himself enjoys and responds to praise, how could we be any different?"

"Praise is the greatest tool in behavior modification," stated B. F. Skinner, leading spokesman of behaviorism. "It goads us to better performance and encourages us to take the risks that expand our lives" (*Redbook*, June 1984).

"I have so often seen people redefine their potential when properly praised and encouraged," psychologist Jonathan Parker, Ph.D., once wrote. "Next to love, I believe it is the greatest gift we can ever give to another!"

The greatest gift . . . next to love? Now what was that about a praise-phrase-craze?

No, the gift of praise can't be waived as just another faddish phase. Surgeons, singers, senators, psychologists, and countless other professionals concur in their experience and opinion! Praise transforms the body, the mind, and the spirit. What other component so positively affects every facet of the human structure? If you have yet to witness the benefits firsthand, learn from the vast experience of others and praise your child to success.

"Seen and Not Heard"?

It was one of the commandments—right up there next to all the other "thou-shalt-nots."

From our earliest recollection, we were reminded that children should be "seen and not heard." As a parent-teacher gimmick to inspire good behavior, it was effective.

But is that *really* what we want? It can't be! Seen-and-not-heard philosophy may account for the many inhibitions and lack of self-expression from which many of us suffer.

Remembering her teaching experience in Georgia's public schools, corporate trainer Linda McElwaney recalled a particular challenge in her classroom:

"Lon was withdrawn, insecure, and very reluctant. He never volunteered in class. Making a special effort to draw him out, I praised any response—right or wrong. By doing so, I built up his self-esteem and helped him to see his response *was* an achievement! Pretty soon, Lon grew more confident and less inhibited. Praise was the key!"

For teachers and other training professionals, it is easy to overlook the hesitant, seen-and-not-heard students in favor of the more verbal, confident ones. Ms. McElwaney understands the importance of healthy, verbal interaction and makes a special effort to include everyone in the learning process.

It's not always performance we should examine so much as progress. Being quick to praise progress at any level will ultimately lead to the performance we want.

Maureen O'Donnell, Virginia's 1983 teacher of the year, affirms, "It is always easy to praise the A student, but I don't have all A students. In my classes are a variety of youngsters. Whether good students or just average, there is some quality, some talent that warrants praise" (*U.S. News and World Report,* September 19, 1983).

We all want a better relationship with our students and children. We hope to respond in a way that makes them feel safe and self-assured. Children must be seen *and* heard! When we tune them out, we miss their message. More importantly, we are unable to decipher the underlying feelings they may be trying to express.

Play fair. Maintain an equal
balance of throw-and-catch
in all your family
communications.

Developing listening skills with a child takes conscious effort. Although we spend 80 percent of our interaction time listening, few of us have mastered the art. Instead of listening, we merely allow someone else a turn to talk.

In his book *How to Speak, How to Listen,* Mortimer J. Adler, Ph.D., compares listening to playing ball. "Catching is as much an activity as throwing and requires as much skill, though it is a skill of a different kind," explains Dr. Adler. "Without the complementary efforts of both players, properly attuned to each other, the play cannot be completed."

Study this page from the "playbook" to help you master the skills of conversational throw-and-catch. Check each statement that best describes your tendencies as a listening parent or teacher.

The more responses you checked, the better listener you're inclined to be. Those statements that did not reflect your current habits indicate areas you can target for improvement.

____ I give my undivided attention, without distraction.

____ I maintain eye contact.

____ I listen with respect, understanding, and empathy.

____ I listen for feelings as well as words.

____ I listen at least as much as I talk.

____ I listen without interruption.

____ I watch and respond to nonverbal signals.

____ I respond calmly in an easy, conversational tone.

____ I repeat the content of his/her message to clarify and summarize our conversation.

____ I talk and listen to my child/student the way I want him/her to talk and listen to me.

FIGURE 3

While listening in the manner described in the checklist, you transmit a clear signal to your child. He hears and *feels* your expression. Allowing him to "throw the ball" as well as "catch it" tells him, *You are important enough for me to take time to under-stand who you are.*

Listening really *talks!* The only effective way to express our inner feelings comes through knowing we are truly understood. A higher standard of learning can only happen as we pursue a higher standard of listening!

Maintain an equal balance of throw-and-catch with all your family players. Don't hog the ball! Play fair. Otherwise, you'll never be a hit at home base. Throwing *and* catching the conversational ball can put your family in the major leagues of quality relationships.

Play ball!

How to Be Fluent
in the Language of "Parent-ese"

Lisa, sixteen, slammed her books on the kitchen table.

"What's wrong with you?" Mom asked.

"Oh, nothing you'd understand," she retorted, escaping to the privacy of her room.

Both experienced silence and hurt feelings. Millions of frustrated parents replay similar scenes every day:

"I'm sick of being treated like a two year old!"

"If you want to be treated like a grown-up, start acting like one!"

"How can I when you keep picking on me all the time?"

Second only to drug concerns, parents are most frustrated about their inability to talk to their children. Out of a thousand girls surveyed by a teen publication, less than one-third confided in their mothers.

Children do things that leave us shaking our heads. Such occasions are frightening and baffling. We want to reach out to help but don't know how. Will we make the problem worse with our awkward attempts to talk? We grope for answers, not always sure of the questions. So what's a parent to do?

Being a successful parent requires that you speak two languages—*yours* and *theirs*. Being your best means knowing when to pay attention to your child as well as reading the real meaning behind his words—or lack of them. Since kids don't always say exactly what they mean, fluency in the language of "parent-ese" helps decipher their true feelings.

With preschoolers, parents can be fairly sure of their child's feelings. Even newborns send an unmistakable message when they are upset, hungry or wet!

The adolescent years present a greater challenge in the art of conversation. Teenagers often communicate with signals rather than words. It's their way of telling you something they cannot express in normal vocabulary. These messages convey a feeling too complex or frightening for them to discuss. Adolescents seem to live on an emotional roller coaster. Because of the wide range of emotions they experience, they often hurt those who are closest to them. And most often that means you—their parent.

Parent-ese is not a dialect you can master in a year or so. Unlike conventional languages, the vocabulary changes. It's an expression of more *emotions,* fewer *words.* Mastery of nouns and verbs is less important than deciphering the emotions masked behind the nouns and verbs.

Confusing, isn't it? Ask any parent.

A first-year parent-ese student may say:

"That's my girl! Such big steps! Now, come to Daddy!"

A six-year parent-ese student will be trying phrases like:

"How was school today? Did you draw this? Great! Let's hang it here on the wall!"

A twelve-year parent will be adding new dialogue such as: "Hi there! Are you home already? Now don't make a mess in the kitchen! Don't throw your books on the table!"

A sixteen-year language student-parent will voice still another stage of expression:

"You left your room in a mess this morning! . . . Now, when I was your age . . . Back in my day . . . Because I said so, and that's final!"

Recognize any patterns here? We don't necessarily get better at this with practice. In the early years, praise crowns our speech. As the child matures, criticism often dominates.

At which stage would *you* feel motivated to try harder? As infants, cheered by the pride and praise of parent-ese, we learn to walk. One hundred percent of us do!

Reassure your child daily:
"I love you no matter
what happens."

How can we overcome the common pitfalls associated with parent-ese expression? One important exercise will help. Learn to think as if you were your child. Try to construct your child's world in your mind. It's a tough assignment. You'll discover your logic is shaded by your own adult perceptions. It will be difficult to think with the immature viewpoint of your child.

Empathy is at work when your inner voice prompts you to ask: *What would make me act the way my child is acting? Why is my child saying this? Why is my child upset?*

Attempting to answer these questions can lead to an understanding and appreciation of your child's silent yet unsteady emotions. And your fluency in parent-ese will soar.

Avoid treating your child like a helpless kid. Although you know what is "right," he must discover some things for himself—even if it means allowing him to make some painful mistakes.

In the real world of parenting, not every sound coming from your lips will be a praise phrase. Real life demands that other words be said. Corrections and instructions, disappointments and frustrations must be addressed. You'll disagree. And occasionally you'll reach your limits. You'll yell a little, fume a little, and forget that the child you're talking to is just that—a child.

You're not perfect. And nobody, not even your child, expects you to be. But he does need you to listen, even to his silence. He expects you to pay attention to his feelings and understand how he views the world. Your gentle understanding and acceptance will go a long way toward helping him sort out his feelings. Fluency in parent-ese will close the communication gap and forge a bond between you.

How's a parent to do all that?

Nobody said it would be easy. Sure we know what's best for our children. We've learned from our experience, and wouldn't it be nice to spare them the pain of making the same mistakes?

Make an effort to develop an attitude, a tone of

voice, empathy, and sincerity that says, *I love you no matter what happens.* Be courageous enough to confide your disappointments, hopes, and feelings in your child. They never grow too old to be told they are loved. Make it a way of life—not just an occasional verbal pat on the head.

Parent-ese translates parental love into action. By putting yourself in your child's shoes, new expression blossoms in your communication. It's the language of a parent's loving heart that brings you closer. And the closer you are to your children, the further they'll be from trouble.

Human Relations 101 and the Ten-Year-Old Professor

Deborah arrived home from work and closed the door behind her. Tension chilled the air. Nicholas, her ten year old, had been in a scuffle with his neighborhood rival, Terry—again. From all accounts, the fault lay with the neighborhood bully. But Mark and Deborah realized Nick must be disciplined since he had been a participant in the tussle.

What does a parent do when these frustrating, and often embarrassing, situations occur? You want to yell a little, scream a little, ship the kid off to reform school, or ground him until he's twenty-one. You hope he'll behave with the manners and social graces of an adult, but it doesn't often happen.

Sure, Mark and Deborah had the same parental urges as most moms and dads. But they also knew that shouting, venting anger, and sending Nick to his room would have little effect on future encounters with the neighborhood bully.

It was then that Mark and Deborah chose to do a very wise and rare thing—perhaps a parental classic.

No whippings. No swats. No harsh rebukes. No demeaning comments. No wisdom-filled rhetoric or sermons. No "now-when-I-was-your-age" kind of lectures. What then?

Nick was instructed to sit down with paper and pencil and list ten things he *liked* about Terry—his neighborhood foe. Ten? How could Nick possibly think of one? Can you imagine a more bitter pill to swallow when all you're feeling are hostile emotions?

And even more painful, Nick was informed that once he completed his "I-like-Terry" list, he must give it to Terry. Who can envision a more distasteful sentence for a feisty, energetic ten year old?

"I can't think of anything!" wailed Nick.

"Well, you can't get up from the table," Deborah firmly advised, "until you come up with at least four tonight."

Finally, Nick settled down to think. Remembering when his leg was broken, Terry had helped him carry his books on the school bus. So he wrote, "Terry is helpful."

> Be alert to the rich, life
> lessons your child
> will teach you.

Thinking about the fun he usually enjoyed in his neighborhood, Nick wrote, "Terry is fun to be around . . . sometimes."

After more fidgeting and soul searching, Nick wrote: "Terry has a good personality."

"Something happened to Nick about this point," recalls Deborah. "It was like a light switched on in Nick's brain as he turned to me and remarked, 'Hey Mom, Terry's really a pretty good friend, isn't he?'"

At this moment Mark and Deborah knew their discipline had worked. And it didn't even require finding ten positives, only three!

"While this incident has not transformed Terry and

Nick into best friends, something far more valuable happened," explains Deborah. "Nick can now recognize there's good to be found in everyone, regardless of how unpleasant or difficult the person may appear to be."

Only a few weeks later, a management shakedown at the office found Deborah facing the prospect of a new boss. Out of three possible candidates, Deborah felt comfortable with two. And the third? Unthinkable! But what were the odds of that happening anyway?

Guess who got the job and became Deborah's new boss? Who else? Mr. Unthinkable!

Her worst fears realized, Deborah spent several stressful days rehearsing all the negative experiences and details she had heard about her new supervisor.

Then like a flashback from the past, Deborah remembered the Nick and Terry incident.

"It was then I realized I could continue to make myself miserable and end up hating my job. Or I could focus on the other side and give it a chance," recalls Deborah.

"I reached for pen and paper and started an 'I-like-Ben' list. What positive qualities does this man possess? What could I possibly like about him? After giving the pen-and-paper test an honest try, my attitude softened.

"And it's been fantastic!" Deborah enthuses. "He's turned out to be the best manager I've ever had . . . totally the opposite of what I imagined. He's supportive. He's been there for me. A great creative thinker!

Turns out the things he's taught me are the areas I needed to grow in anyway!"

What brought about the transformation in Nick? In Deborah? Did the neighborhood bully undergo drastic behavior modification? Did Deborah's new boss manage any differently?

No. The difference sprang from their own decisions to direct their focus in a new way—a positive one! There is so much good in the worst of us and so much bad in the best of us that it hardly makes sense for any of us to focus negatively on ourselves and others. Sure, it's there, and plenty of it. But so is the good. Resolve now to begin seeing others in a fresh, new, and positive perspective. By doing so, you can change the destiny and direction of your life—and that of your children!

The only thing more important than what you pour *into* your child is what comes *out*—the product or fruit of your parental efforts! No greater legacy can you bestow for equipping your child to survive and succeed than to grant him the ability to focus positively on his world!

You're right, this is not a brilliant, new concept. Actually, it's one of the core basics of getting along in this world: Human Relations 101. Yet often in our pursuit of a higher standard of learning, we can benefit from a rousing review of the basics. We forget. We get busy. We overlook the obvious in pursuit of something more lofty, profound, and advanced.

Through this series of incidents, Mark and Deborah reaped one of the priceless rewards of parenthood. In the continuous flow of encouraging, teaching, worrying, cajoling, and fussing, we are astounded when—in a phenomenal reversal of roles—our children become teachers and we, their students.

If it hasn't happened already to you, like it did to Deborah, it will, and when you least expect it. Somewhere along the endless stream of parenting, your child strides to the front of the classroom, chalk in hand, and opens the textbook to illustrate a truth as only a master teacher can do. And at the same time, you slip back into your old school desk unawares, pen in hand, and open your notebook to learn from the wise, yet innocent professor—your child!

Hey, Nick! Don't tell your mom and dad just yet, but someday they'll realize you've been the best teacher they ever had!

12 Strokes for Painting a Happy Child Portrait

Monet. Renoir. Van Gogh.

What vivid impressions come to mind? Why do we still revere and appreciate their art more than a century later?

As prominent artists from the Impressionist era, they painted with a unique style of short, swift strokes of pure prismatic colors. Each canvas was composed of countless distinct, deliberate brush strokes. The real beauty of their skill could be appreciated even more from a distance—allowing the eye to blend the strokes for a pleasing effect.

As a parent, you have joined the elite club of the Impressionists. By simple virtue of your offspring, you've earned the job. The challenge is to make a positive, vibrant, and lasting impression. Child development experts have concluded that the timing of praise is critical. What matters most is when and how strokes are applied.

Apply the dozen strokes offered here for producing a happy child portrait. Since verbal and nonverbal strokes define your child's world, take out your palette and brush to paint a vivid, stroke-filled masterpiece worthy of the gallery.

Offer a Positive Praise Phrase

Phrase your applause carefully so that children don't get mixed signals. Don't quip, "How nice to see you being good for a change," or "You got all As— great! Now if you'd only do that every time!"

As an Impressionist, select colors from your palette that are complementary. Clashing hues don't mix well here. Children are puzzled and frustrated upon hearing such a mixed review.

Here, the praise reflects a judgment which conveys quite the opposite of what was intended. Your applause should be designed to strengthen his behavior, not to confuse him.

A child cannot feel encouraged if his teacher or parent praises and criticizes in the same breath. Praise must stand alone with nothing to mar its brilliance.

Be Immediate and Specific

Dr. Mike Wronkovich, Ohio school principal, underlines the importance of *immediate* praise:

> I visited the classroom of one of my teachers, Craig, who was well-known for his success in the classroom. Initially, I was puzzled. Craig was not a particularly great speaker. His lessons were not full of fire. He was certainly no entertainer. I had to wonder how he could achieve such success while appearing so bland. In searching deeper and observing more frequently, I discovered that this man knew exactly when to praise his students at the optimum time!

Praise should occur immediately after the worthy act. Immediate praise emphasizes more clearly the kind of behavior that's expected—and will be rewarded.

Just as praise must be immediate, it should be

specific. If a child is granted blanket approval or if every act is applauded with "that's wonderful, that's great," she will have no clue what she's actually able to do.

As an Impressionist, save your abstract art for another canvas. Child strokes must be well-defined, distinct, and realistic. Praise should be connected to specific behavior. Allow your child to understand exactly what is evoking your approval: "You did a good job of putting your toys away so neatly." Then she gets a sense of herself as an orderly, organized person.

Rather than muttering a vague approval, restate the behavior just performed and use it as a teaching moment. You might say, "Thank you for putting the dishes away. When we work together, we finish sooner and have more time to spend in the park."

Specific and immediate feedback is essential for children. Now's the time to "brush up" with specifics.

Give More You's, Less I's

The parental role is not for sitting in judgment. Allow your child the privilege of evaluating and relishing his own accomplishments.

"I'm so proud of you," sounds positive enough. But the accent is on the wrong person—on the *I* of the phrase, rather than on *you*. What the child has accomplished sounds only important from the perspective of what "I" think of it. It reeks with a patronizing big-I-little-you kind of tone.

A more favorable approach might be: "You must be so pleased you made it all by yourself!"

In addition to the positive reinforcement you offer, encourage your child to internalize good feelings for his own accomplishments. "Way to go! Your project is finished with time to spare. How does that make you feel?" Such direction encourages the child to think about himself in positive ways that nurture self-esteem.

Praise Them to "Follow Through"

"Last night Phil had put off doing his homework until the last minute," relates his dad, Justin. "He was stalling to avoid finishing it.

"I told him, 'Phil, you've done such a good job with your homework until now, you deserve a lot of credit for hanging in there. A little extra push, and you'll be finished. You must be really pleased to have completed all of this!'

"Well, Phil got busy and did it. He was really happy with himself! Eventually he will learn to give himself the extra nudge to follow through on other challenging tasks."

Children lose interest in activities quickly. Your praise—like Justin's—can motivate your child to complete what he has started.

Establish a Safe, Supportive Environment

Create a classroom or home environment that convinces children they are welcome and accepted as they are. Often children are paralyzed by fear that others will laugh or ridicule them. When parents and teachers create an atmosphere that is safe and supportive, children are more apt to participate and learn.

Firmly establish ground rules up front that you will not tolerate put-downs and negative comments about others. Take time to illustrate why put-downs are so damaging. Whenever a negative comment surfaces, be quick to defend your "no put-downs" policy. Be cautious that your own example is a positive one as well.

As children grow older, it is important to protect and respect their need for privacy. It is often difficult to realize they sometimes need to be alone to sort things out. Your carefully guarded turf will become a haven for thriving confidence, trust, and self-esteem.

Look for Good in Their Mistakes

Lucy, the famous cartoon philosopher, appears on the baseball diamond to counsel a distraught player after another humiliating loss. "We learn more from losing," she proclaims, "than we do from winning." In the next frame, a frantic Charlie Brown throws up his hands and concedes, "That makes me about the smartest person in the world!"

The unconventional wisdom of Charlie Brown provides a lesson for parents. Look for the good in your child's mistakes and losses. Help him view his errors and mishaps as a golden opportunity to learn a new lesson and improve himself. Minimizing mistakes will help him accept the unpleasant consequences that often accompany his blunders.

Talk to your child about some of your own fumbles. Laugh about them together and point out the lessons you learned as a result. Then look for something you can praise in his oops-kind-of-moments. By doing so, you encourage your child to realize mistakes are okay and should be accepted as a normal part of learning, living and growing.

Love Them Anyway!

Loads of affection, both physical and verbal, are essential for well-adjusted kids. However, don't make your kids earn your approval and affection. Your love should never be contingent upon good behavior or achievement. Let your kids know that even when you object to their behavior, you still love them. The ability to separate the actions from the person is primary. Successful parenting requires you to assert positive feelings about your children while taking proper action to correct their mistakes.

> Be an Impressionist! Apply
> frequent strokes to create
> a parent's masterpiece.

Assure your children that you accept them as they are—their good moments and their bad, their strengths and their weaknesses. Avoid pressuring your kids to measure up to your image or that of siblings or neighbors. True parental love allows your children the freedom to be unique.

React with "Yes" Instead of "No"

"I made a real effort to praise Nicole and avoid saying 'no' so often," explains her mom, Sue Ellen.

"When she pulled the dog's ears, I ignored it. When she didn't, I praised her for being kind and gentle with the pet. It took a lot of patience on my part (and the dog's), but it was worth it."

"If you glow at what you like, the *absence* of the glow says what you don't like," explains Dr. Sirgay Sanger, a New York child psychiatrist. "Wait until your daughter doesn't spill her food; *then* praise her for neatness."

Ten-year-old Jeremy was helping his mom dry dishes after dinner. Wiping a large platter, he lost his grip and the heavy dish shattered on the floor.

Silence.

His mother chose this suspense-filled moment to say "yes" rather than "no."

"You know, Jeremy, of all the times you have wiped dishes for me, this is the first time you dropped one. I think you have set some kind of record!"

Anxiety drained from the boy's face as he smiled broadly. As a result, both Jeremy and his mom enjoyed a positive moment.

Create Opportunities for Praising

In our desire to be good parents, we often overdo it. Too many parents burden themselves by doing things for their kids they could be doing for themselves—cleaning their rooms, packing their lunch, doing their own laundry—the list goes on. Structure situations within your home or classroom to allow children to experience good feelings about their capabilities. Allow them the opportunity to experience accountability through meaningful, "do-able" jobs.

Wise parents and teachers delegate responsibility—then praise the accomplishment. What better way to boost self-esteem, confidence, and maturity! Make them feel their contributions are significant and important. Create an environment in which your child *can* experience success.

Give yourself a break. Let them do it, then praise them for it!

Praise by Total Involvement

"What a grand tower you've built with your blocks!"

Examine two different parents saying these same words. Parent A walks by, makes the statement in an offhand, detached manner. The parent's true interest and attention are elsewhere.

Parent B makes the same comment with lively, enthusiastic expression. He stops and expands the encounter by asking questions. "How did you do that? Do you enjoy building things? What else have you built?"

Consider the two approaches. Draw—no, paint—your own conclusions. The parent involved with his child expresses his desire to communicate. And the child translates this attention to mean affection, love and favor.

"I still remember my mother's response to a bouquet I had picked for her birthday," recalls Fredelle Maynard in a 1988 *Woman's Day* article. "All I'd been able to find were a few violets, some buttercups, and a single crumpled daisy. My mother did not exclaim over the beauty of the blossoms; she just brought out her best crystal vase, arranged my flowers as carefully as if they were long-stemmed roses, sniffed the buttercups appreciatively—and gave me a big hug. That was praise indeed."

What a perfect example of praise by total involvement!

Both Parents Must Praise

Remember, your masterpiece is a joint venture. It requires strokes from the brushes of many artists. Although your child is the focal point of the portrait, the background is an essential part of the composition. As parents, *you* provide the background.

Because praise is an expression of love, it is important that your child hear it from both Mom and Dad. Hearing it from two sources strengthens and validates the praise.

If Dad isn't comfortable offering praise just yet, work him into it easily. Arrange to have him present when Mom gives it. While telling your daughter her grades were outstanding, Mom can add, "And Dad feels the same!" That way, Dad can follow up with a grin, hug, handshake, or a "Way to go!"

Are you a single parent? Ask a friend or relative of the opposite sex to join your praise-giving efforts. "Just wait until Grandpa sees this! He'll be pleased!"

Have Fun with It!

There are countless ways to provide other positive feedback. Create special occasions for giving recognition to your child.

Keep memories alive with photographs. Praise celebrations need not be elaborate. Children love the fun and fuss of rituals and remember them long after you have forgotten.

Recognize achievement or progress with awards, badges, or stickers. A simple cutout handprint attached to the child's shoulder illustrates a nifty pat on the back. And his visible "trophy" allows him to share his achievement with peers and parents.

One woman presents a special toast to a deserving family member at dinner. A man I know treats his sons to a little masculine respect with a hug and a handshake, followed by the brothers' exchanging high-fives.

A busy mother of three mounted an Appreciation Bulletin Board in her kitchen. Every time a family member achieves something praiseworthy, she posts it on the board. When daughter Sarah brought home an A in math, Mom displayed the test paper on the board. Other trophies included Jeff's perfect dental check-up and a newspaper clipping featuring Jeremy's little league victory.

A creative father designed wall charts for his twin sons to document their progress on assigned chores such as cleaning their rooms, brushing their teeth, or feeding the pets.

Such creative forms of praise, coupled with your

verbal approval, allow your child the sense of accomplishment of seeing as well as hearing your applause.

Too often, we tend to reward the *result* while forgetting to reward the *effort*. As you continue the art of stroking, evaluate your progress at regular intervals. This will make you aware of how daily, minor efforts have led to major results. Such summary can remind both of you to feel good about how far you've come!

At birth, your child came as a blank canvas. You've provided the best possible palette and brush, the finest frame and easel. But *none* of these accessories makes your project a work of art. What counts is what's on the canvas!

Don't doodle your way through, leaving a sketchy, abstract impression. Apply the color, the expression, the stroking—and lots of it! As your child matures, you'll back off and view the pleasing effect from a distance with a parent's pride.

Like many of the Impressionists, your work may not be fully appreciated today or next year or the next. But the full effect of your loving skill will remain etched for a lifetime in the image of your child!

Now you get the picture!

You Gotta Do Your "Homework" to Pass the PPQ!

It was one of those things every good kid did. It was the dividing line, separating the good from the bad. It reeked with diligence and responsibility. You *had* to do your homework! Those who didn't ranked right up there next to the sneering, leering Post Office poster faces.

> Do your homework! Target and review your child's strengths with him regularly.

Well, homework isn't just for kids anymore. Are *you* doing your homework? You must frequently identify and review your child's strengths with her.

Just *how* good are you? What is your PPQ (Parent Praise Quotient)? To find out, review the following ten statements. Each positive response yields ten points to your total PPQ score.

___ I have personally praised my child for a specific achievement or act within the past three days.

___ I can readily identify my child's greatest strength.

___ I frequently make my child feel important as an integral part of our family unit.

Continued on the following page

_____ I avoid comparing my child's achievements and strengths with those of siblings or other children.

_____ I frequently ask my child for his/her opinion or input.

_____ I give my child the courtesy of listening just as I do with others outside my family.

_____ I am involved in my child's education. I meet with my child's teacher regularly to discuss his/her progress, abilities, challenges, potential, etc.

_____ I assure my child he/she is loved, even when his/her actions are unacceptable.

_____ I recognize my child's own special talents and strengths, even if they are not reflected on his/her report card.

_____ I have spent quality time in conversation and/or activity with my child in the past twenty-four hours.

Total Score _____

FIGURE 4

101 Ways to Phrase Your Praise
(Without Saying "Great!")

"You really made a difference by . . ."

"That's the way to . . ."

"I appreciate your help with . . ."

"That's a valid point of . . ."

"You made a real accomplishment when you . . ."

"That's very perceptive of you to . . ."

"That took a lot of patience when you . . ."

"You're right on the mark with . . ."

"Do you always do such a thorough job of . . . ?"

"I'm impressed with your . . ."

"You're on the right track by . . ."

"That's the best you've ever done with . . ."

"You really applied yourself when you . . ."

"You really went all out when you . . ."

"You've come a long way on this by . . ."

"That's quite an achievement the way you . . ."

"You know, you're pretty terrific because you . . ."

"You got my attention when you . . ."

"It took a lot of courage on your part when you . . ."

"You've got what it takes to . . ."

"Your efforts really pay off when you . . ."

"You're making a lot of headway with . . ."

"One of the things I enjoy most about you is . . ."

"You're doing top-quality work on . . ."

"I admire you for . . ."

"Your hard work really paid off because of your . . ."

"Your success is showing because you . . ."

"You're really impressive when you . . ."

"You really stick with it the way you . . ."

"Your persistence paid off by . . ."

"This tells me how much you care . . ."

"Way to go with . . ."

"You're a tough act to follow because of your . . ."

"You're coming along precisely with . . ."

"This is first-class work on . . ."

"That was a real breakthrough when you . . ."

"You can be proud of yourself for . . ."

"Outstanding job of . . ."

"You outdid yourself by . . ."

"I'm learning a lot from your . . ."

"You deserve a lot of credit for your . . ."

"What a lot of progress on . . ."

"You really did the job by . . ."

"You proved you could do it by . . ."

"You've made my day because you . . ."

"You're really on top of things . . ."

"I like your style of . . ."

"I see a lot of improvement in your . . ."

"Your determination is evident because you . . ."

"You must feel really pleased about your . . ."

"You've won our respect by . . ."

"Looks like a winner because of your . . ."

"You have a special talent for . . ."

"I admire the way you take the time to . . ."

"You've won our recognition by . . ."

"You made it with flying colors because you . . ."

"You're a winner because you . . ."

"You've done it again by . . ."

"We couldn't have done it without your . . ."

"You've got my admiration because of your . . ."

"I enjoy working with you because of your . . ."

"You really know how to . . ."

"I'm with you all the way on . . ."

"What an effective way to . . ."

"I know I can count on you because . . ."

"You're really going places with . . ."

"You've got the right idea of . . ."

"No one could have done a better job of . . ."

"Now, that's what we're looking for!"

"You're on your way up because you . . ."

"You've made it all the way by . . ."

"This shows a lot of confidence on your part because you . . ."

Qualify your praise with specifics for maximum impact.

"Now, that's the way to . . ."

"That's the best job of _____ I've ever seen!"

"You have a special gift for . . ."

"Looks like a professional job of . . ."

"Now you're getting the idea of . . ."

"We applaud your efforts to . . ."

"My hat is off to you for . . ."

"I salute the job you've done here because . . ."

"Repeat performance of . . ."

"Of course you'll do a stellar job of . . ."

"Look how far you've come with . . ."

"You really helped me when you . . ."

"We're a better team because of your . . ."

"I appreciate how you . . ."

"You're so much fun to be with because you . . ."

"Well done job of . . ."

"We're all pleased with the way you . . ."

"I like working with you because of your . . ."

"You're doing a first-rate job of . . ."

"It's a pleasure watching a pro like you because you . . ."

"You display a winner's attitude every time you . . ."

"I see real leadership in your . . ."

"You're really going strong with . . ."

"You add so much _____ to the success of our group . . ."

"You're pretty special because you . . ."

"You know, you're famous for . . ."

"I'm glad you're on my team because you . . ."

"I believe in you because you . . ."

"Is this quality stuff or what?"

Could Praise Have Changed History?

His were all the tragic trappings of a broken home. Mom married three times. Dad died two months before his son's birth.

Until age four, he was shifted in and out of an orphanage. His widowed mother worked long hours to support her three sons—but not without resentment. "We learned, very early, that we were a burden," one son later recalled. She afforded little time for attention, affection, praise, or consistent discipline during her sons' formative years. Instead, she embittered them and turned them against her.

As an adolescent, he was a loner. Girls ignored him. Boys cruelly taunted him about his clothes, his mannerisms, and his accent. Slight and scrawny, he spoke with a squeaky voice.

Even with a high IQ, he received no encouragement to achieve or excel academically. Eventually, he became a high school drop-out.

Seeking the adventure, pride, and self-respect depicted in the recruitment posters, he joined the Marine Corps at age seventeen. They claimed to be looking for a few good men. Would he find acceptance here? Even there, happiness eluded him. Fellow Marines jeered and humiliated him. Fighting back, he became disruptive and defied authority. He was court-martialed and later discharged.

Escaping his problems, he travelled halfway around the world and settled in another country. He married and later brought his wife to America.

Nothing changed. Soon his wife fell victim to his

erratic behavior and threatened to leave him. As he shifted from one mediocre job to another, one shabby apartment to another, his marriage began to unravel. His young wife and family needed things he could not provide. Frustrated, he became erratically violent and abusive. Eventually, he and his wife separated.

Attempting to make it on his own, he failed miserably. After days of loneliness, he returned and wept on his knees, pleading with his wife to let him come home. Stripped of his self-respect and dignity, he crawled back.

Recognize that the presence
or absence of your
encouragement may spell
the difference between
triumph and tragedy.

Tenderhearted, he wept when a family friend surprised him with a cake for his twenty-fourth birthday. He wept again a few days later when his second daughter was born.

Finally, he resigned to the bitter inner struggle. No one needed—or even wanted—him. It seemed no one had *ever* wanted him. Unloved, undesirable, he was easily impressionable. All of his life he had fervently crusaded for a cause, for acknowledgment and recognition—yet with little success. Hungry for acceptance, he possibly fell victim to the designs of more powerful forces. And he may well have been the greatest human tragedy of our century.

One winter morning, he awoke a strangely different man. At long last, would he find the recognition, the acceptance he so passionately sought? With a new resolve, he set out for his $1.25-an-hour job at the book storage building.

Could a friend's praise have changed his direction? Could he have been dissuaded from his momentous mission with a kind word or a loving embrace? Might his life have taken a happier course—free of the suspicions and allegations that continue to shroud him? The world will never know.

Looking out from a sixth floor window that November afternoon, *many believe* he fired two fatal bullets into the head of the President of the United States.

The Home Team Wins

Children don't require perfection. What they need most is what Lee Harvey Oswald sought and sadly never received. Regardless of his guilt or innocence, his brief twenty-four years bear tragic evidence of the absence of self-esteem and loving encouragement.

Children need us to go ahead of them, clearing the path, marking the boundaries, and directing their progress. They count on us to recognize and discover their potential and to coach them. They depend on us to make the goals clear. And when they experience success, shouting, "Hey! Look what I did!" they expect us to verify their victory.

Yes, it takes *everyone* working together to ensure a victory for the home team! Remember, you're all on the same side—teammates—not opponents. When your children succeed, you are a winner also.

Renowned minister and author Dr. Charles Allen recalled to me his "home team" with warm affection: "I was so blessed to grow up in a home where I felt love instead of criticism. In my earliest years as a minister, my father, also a minister, never once criticized my sermons. I am still inspired by him!"

In this business of parenting, teaching, or coaching, praise is not a part-time, sometime thing. Rather, it is a continual process. The supreme goal is to develop a person who no longer depends solely on the opinion of others but who can set his own ideals having grown confident in his own accomplishments. Secure in his ability, he can believe the world is his.

Together, you score a smashing victory for the home team!

FOUR

Pursue a Higher Standard of Loving

◆

"Your success as a family, our
success as a society, depends not
on what happens at the White
House, but on what happens
inside your house."

Former First Lady, Barbara Bush

◆

Chapter Objectives

○ Remember, you don't just have a job, you have a life.

○ Neglect the whole world rather than each other.

○ Come to listen. Come to learn. Come to *life!*

○ Sprinkle some intimate me-to-you magic in all your love expressions.

○ Explore and practice new ways of saying "I love you."

○ Extend your life and your love with generous hugs and kisses.

○ Ask yourself: *What would my life be like without him?*

○ Give her a daily "heart-piece" to make your love a lifelong masterpiece.

Eleven months had elapsed since Keith and Karyn's glitzy church wedding—complete with all the Cinderella trimmings. The starry-eyed couple beamed like Barbie and Ken personified. Everything was perfect. The union held all the promise of a sugar-icing finish!

"So how's married life?" I asked good-naturedly upon greeting Keith at the airport almost a year later.

The sharp reality of matrimonial existence had settled in—hard.

"Well, we've got the ever-after part down real good," he said, half-jokingly. "Who knows what happens to the happy stuff?"

What *does* happen to the "happily ever after" part? In a country where forty percent of the best-selling book market is romantic fiction, why can't we create a little nonfiction happiness of our own?

We can! And that's what this section of the book is set to reveal.

"How do I look?" she asks.

"Fine," he mumbles.

"Why won't you ever talk to me?" she challenges.

"But I *am* talking to you right now!" he retorts.

Heard any of these lines? Anywhere familiar—like maybe in *your* living room?

Would you describe your relationship with the glow and glamour of Barbie and Ken? Or more like the glare and gloom of Edith and Archie? It's amazing how that fresh glow of love can fade like yesterday's news when the reality of just-the-two-of-us-together-forever ultimately sinks in.

There is no arena where praise is more appreciated, or less likely offered, than in our love relationships. In the ordinary continuity of daily life, our insights often are blurred. Assets are taken for granted and we forget to appreciate those we love most. Minor aggravations are magnified so that we seem less like lovers and more like a pair of crotchety roommates.

People at random are generally not reliable sources for gaining positive strokes. So we create relationships. While we form relationships to enjoy continual stroking and positive feelings, too often we forget the ingredients that nourished the relationship into being.

Funny, isn't it? When the two of you fell in love, you clung to each other like super glue. You were convinced that half the love songs were written just for the pair of you! There was never enough time to be together.

Time usually changes those wonderful, dizzy days of head-over-heels infatuation. We become accustomed to each other and fail to notice the positives in our partner. Once we were swept off our feet by romance; now our relationships may soon be swept into the dustpan.

Sometimes we get accustomed to the good things in life. Eventually, we convince ourselves that we even deserve them! The absence of praise and loving expressions warns that your relationship is under strain or that negative feelings are accumulating. Read your crucial patterns as critical signs. You're waving a red flag at your mate just as surely as if you were a matador.

Unconsciously, we wait for good feelings to return before we begin expressing our love or praise. But how else can we revive the good feelings unless we trigger them first? Take responsibility for tendering your love rather than waiting for your partner to take the initiative.

The alert partner who initiates those reassuring remarks at just the right time is insuring against the challenges that threaten every relationship.

Ask yourself, *Am I living "happily," or just "ever after?"* No, you don't need a glass slipper or a pumpkin coach to make it happen. Actually it takes much more. Are you first willing to *give* more than you *get* in your pursuit of a higher, happier standard of loving?

Way to Go, Barbara!

When Wellesley College scheduled a commencement speaker for its 1990 graduation, Barbara Bush was second choice. Some Wellesley seniors questioned whether Mrs. Bush was an appropriate role model for today's modern woman.

"To honor Barbara Bush as commencement speaker," they protested, "is to honor a woman who has gained recognition through the achievements of her husband, which contradicts what we have been taught the past four years."

> Remember, you don't just
> have a job, you have a life.

Mrs. Bush was neither offended nor intimidated by their protests. And without apology for her own traditional values, the First Lady offered this advice in her commencement address:

Cherish your human connections, your relationships with friends and family. For several years, you've had impressed upon you the importance to your career of dedication and hard work.

This is true, but as important as your obligations as a doctor, lawyer, or business leader will be, you are a human being *first* and those human connections—with spouses, with children, with friends—are the most important investments you will ever make.

At the end of your life, you will never regret not

having passed one more test, not winning one more verdict, or not closing one more deal. You *will* regret time not spent with a husband, a friend, a child, or a parent.

The First Lady's advice underlines the most valuable principle in this book. Achieving a higher standard of living, leading, or learning is indeed a worthy pursuit. Yet none of these should be the *most* important.

Our loving relationships and "human connections" nourish our spirits and give meaning to our lives. Without these, all other accomplishments are diminished. It's like giving the performance of a lifetime to the echo of an empty hall!

Too often, we lose sight of what is really important. The rush that comes from closing a high-dollar deal or earning a long-sought degree has an appeal that mounds of dirty diapers and dinner dishes do not. Society says the only goals worth pursuing are those that come with a paycheck attached. We've concluded that the only accomplishments worth mastering are the ones that enhance our résumés.

Human relationships are hard work. That's the reason so many fail when difficulties surface. Relationships are high risk. They are also high reward— the highest reward—and the closest we can come to happiness, contentment, and fulfillment.

Regardless of the priorities forced on us by a get-ahead-any-way-you-can society, don't expend all of your energies in pursuit of career goals. What you do for a living is not *all* there is to you. Remember, you don't just have a job, you have a life! Get on with discovering your numerous multifaceted dimensions.

Love has not gone out of style. Our "human connections" are still the *most* important.

Way to go, Barbara!

If He Could Hear
What She Cannot Say

It wasn't the apple on the tree but rather the "pair" on the ground that caused all the chaos in Paradise. Ever since the Garden of Eden, male-female relationships have suffered frequent communication tangles.

She longs to tell you how she really feels but she doesn't. He wants to tell you what he really means but he can't. It's a perplexing dilemma common to most relationships.

We are much like Max, who exclaimed to his wife, Marge, "Sometimes, dear, when I think about how much you mean to me, I can hardly keep from telling you!"

Dr. Nathaniel Branden, author of the amazing book *If You Could Hear What I Cannot Say,* offers help for couples struggling to voice their feelings. Director of the Biocentric Institute in Beverly Hills, Dr. Branden has developed a unique sentence-completion system that stimulates hesitant partners to verbalize hidden emotions.

When couples arrive for counseling, the pair sits facing each other. One partner remains silent while the other responds to Branden's verbal technique.

Branden instructs his client to complete the sentence: "*One of the things I want from you and don't know how to ask for is. . .*"

Repeating the partial statement, Branden encourages his client to fill in the blank with at least six completions, and if he gets stuck—invent. Six? Sure, it can be a stretch for some of us. Typical responses might reveal such disclosures as "more of your time . . . more attention . . . more intimate conversation."

After several revealing statements, the silent partner responds similarly: "*As I sit here listening to you, I. . .*"

Responses may uncover such expressions as "I realize we make the same mistakes . . . I understand why we miss each other . . . I want us to be more truthful with each other."

"If you want to improve communication in your marriage," explains Dr. Branden, "the key is to stop assuming that your partner can read your mind; instead, take responsibility for transmitting what you want him to know, happy news as well as bad.

"Couples who remain deeply in love frequently say 'I love you' (or equivalents) and often reiterate what they admire and enjoy about each other. They understand the nurturing power of communication."

Branden suggests his technique be used for defining problem areas and also for offering appreciation. Even if you enjoy a marriage made in heaven, the maintenance work must be done here on Earth.

Minus the services of a professional, try this exercise for expressing the good in each other. Face your partner and take turns talking. Switch roles.

If either of you is uncomfortable responding verbally, write out your answers. Complete these phrases to spark new appreciation with your partner:

- *One of the qualities I admire in you is . . .*
- *One of the things I love about our relationship is . . .*
- *One of the things I'll always be grateful to you for is . . .*

- *The longer I know you, the more I love you for . . .*
- *When I'm away from you, one thing I miss most is . . .*
- *One of your achievements I'm really proud of is . . .*
- *One of the nicest things you ever said to me is . . .*
- *One of the traits that first attracted me to you is . . .*
- *One of my favorite memories of us together is . . .*
- *I feel closest to you when we . . .*

Once the lines of communication unclog and flow freely, employ the same technique to open other new avenues into your relationship.

Lovers often probe for ways to express their love, never knowing specifically what pleases their partner most. So now's your chance to find out.

Neglect the whole world rather than each other.

Here's how: List several desirable actions that your mate does, that she could do, or that you wish she would do that would make you feel more appreciated, nurtured, or special.

It's okay. Indulge yourself! Choose your "wish list" carefully. Avoid general terms like *consideration, love, respect,* etc. Think specifically. *Exactly* what would you like to see happen?

Complete this statement describing ten precise actions: "*I feel your love and care every time you . . .*"

Actions on your wish list might include ". . . ask me about my day . . . kiss me good-bye in the morning . . . call me during the day . . . hold my hand when we're out together . . . surprise me with a card or love note just because . . ."

Once you're finished, exchange lists. Read them carefully. Clarify all details to avoid misunderstanding. Discuss, edit, and add more ideas borrowed from your companion's list.

This business of relationships is an ongoing, perpetual challenge. Like any living thing, your love demands deliberate effort, attention and maintenance. Is it worth it? Yes! Is there *anything else* in the world more important?

Among her dozen gems for keeping a happy marriage, Ann Landers advises, "Neglect the whole world rather than each other." Your wish list is just one more way to prevent neglect from creeping in on your partnership!

Keep your mate's list in full view on your mirror, dashboard, briefcase, desk . . . wherever you'll be seeing it frequently. Set a daily goal of expressing your love with at least two of the requested actions. Challenge each other to see who can fulfill the most wishes for the other within a week.

Thanks to your wish list, you will soon be experiencing focused, deliberate attention from your lover. Relish the feeling! Now you have specific reason to utilize your PraisePower by appreciating your partner even further. What a wonderful, exhilarating cycle to keep your passions alive!

Now, why didn't Adam and Eve think of this? If they had spent *more* time talking and *less* time munching apples . . . .

What to Do When All He Says Is "Huh?"

"Randall, I'm leaving you for another man."

"Huh? Uh, . . . fine, hon, I'll be ready in a minute."

It's amazing how we've conditioned ourselves to respond to our partners when we're not really tuned in.

Just what are you supposed to do when all he (or she) says is "huh?" As a species, Homo sapiens don't seem to have progressed far beyond the prehistoric era when grunts and groans were the chief means of exchange.

Though the major thrust of this book underlines positive self-expression, *real* communication is a two-way street. How effective can our words be if we are not in touch with each other? Knowing your partner's temperament and mood is as elementary as knowing your own address. Without either, you can't go home again.

Listening to someone you've lived with a long time can be difficult. You can't help thinking you know in advance what the other person is going to say. It's that here-we-go-again reflex. After years together, you can finish each other's sentences, right?

Improve your listening skills with your partner. Try on these "hearing aids" for a better fit in your relationship.

Tune in to Your Partner's Feelings

Be attentive to your partner. Be sensitive to your partner's feelings and create an atmosphere of unconditional love. Avoid interrupting, giving advice, or passing judgment. Avoid telling your mate *why* he shouldn't feel this way. Don't try to be the savior for his problems.

The best way to keep from stepping on your partner's toes is to put yourself in your partner's shoes. Try 'em on!

Resist Distractions

Not since Noah's ark has it made so much sense to get away from it all two-by-two. Make it a regular practice to go where you can't be distracted—a weekend getaway, a restaurant—somewhere to make quality, undistracted time for your partnership.

Intense listening in a family setting is impossible. When tuning in your partner, be aware of external distractions that compete for your attention—the kids, the telephone, the television, and a hundred and one domestic duties.

Yielding to such distractions during conversation sends your partner a negative message: *What's going on here is more important to me than what you're saying.*

"Mirror" Your Partner

When you do respond, resist the urge to talk about yourself or your ideas first. Instead, repeat or "mirror" what you've heard from her.

Suppose she lashes out: "The kids are driving me nuts! There's never any peace and quiet around this place!"

Rather than striking back with a rebuttal, mirror

her complaint: "You seem upset. You don't feel like you're getting enough space around here, am I right?"

Winning her agreement initially increases your chances at making progress. If you ignore your partner's emotions, she will feel neglected and the chance for communication is lost.

Come to *Listen*

Sure, *hold* a conversation with your mate, but let go of it now and then. We may assume our mates want advice just because they ask for it. More often, what they *really* want is a sympathetic ear and a chance to talk it out. Save your advice. Resist slipping into your first-I'll-listen-then-I'll-give-you-my-advice kind of mode.

"After thirty-six years," reveals Ann Landers, "I realize that many people who write to me don't want advice. They just need someone who will listen."

There's a great difference between having to say something and having something to say. Avoid offering the benefit of your wisdom if you sense he needs to talk about it. Come to the table—not to negotiate—simply to *listen*.

Come to *Learn*

Skillful listening can be the most valuable growth experience in your relationship. Ask yourself, *What can I learn here about my partner that I may have overlooked?*

Ask questions carefully. Questions can perpetuate

a conversation. They can also kill it. The difference is in the skill of the questioner.

In male-female conversations, *she* asks most of the questions. Women view questions as an effective way to keep a conversation alive. Men tend to view questions as requests for information.

Come to listen. Come to learn. Come to *life!*

Men are less apt to ask personal questions. They rationalize, *If she wants me to know something, then she'll tell me.* A woman reasons, *If I don't ask, he'll think I don't care.*

Come to *Life!*

"You're not listening to a word I've said!" Marianne accuses her husband.

"I can repeat every single word you've said," Mike retorts.

Avoid the ugly dialogue. Offer your companion an attentive "yeah" or "uh-huh" now and then to prove you're not comatose and you're still tuned in. Women are especially adept at using facial expression and gestures to illustrate their interest. Men often have to work harder at practicing an active body language that says, *I'm conscious and interested in what you're saying.*

You've read the ways for doing it. Now implement. Hearing is not the same as listening. You heard her (or him) when you said "huh?" Hearing is a passive act; it happens because you have ears.

Listening is an active pursuit that requires skill, patience, energy, and much practice. Yet it is one of the most sincere expressions of caring for your lover. Come to listen. Come to learn. Come to life!

Factor in a higher law of mathematics to formulate the lover's perfect equation: The act of true listening equals the act of true loving. Happy listening and loving!

When You Dare Enough
to Say Your Very Best

When teenager Joyce Clyde Hall stepped off the train in Kansas City in 1910, he could not have known the impact he would make on human expression over the next century.

Inside his suitcase were two shoe boxes of picture postcards. Inside his head was a plan for distributing them. The business he went on to develop from his room at the YMCA has mushroomed into Hallmark Cards, Inc.—the multi-billion dollar, undisputed king of the ever-expanding greeting card industry.

More than anyone else, Joyce Hall was the architect of the greeting card enterprise. He established a social custom that shows no sign of subsiding. Hallmark now has plenty of company. More than a thousand other greeting card companies currently produce cards in the United States. Consumers spend five billion dollars to buy seven billion cards each year.

Just how do they do it? Composing expressions that convey our true feelings is difficult. Too often the fear of sounding awkward paralyzes us.

Avoid the easy way out. Let's practice, using a few tips from the industry pros in becoming more expressive in the language of love:

Say What You Feel

Use comfortable language. Don't attempt to say something that doesn't fit your style. Greeting card designers seek to fit your personal manner of expression. Now, more than ever, a variety of greeting cards is available for all tastes and sentiments. You can even buy attractive blank cards and create your own.

No matter how attractive the illustration, marketing analysts insist consumers refuse to buy a card that doesn't communicate what they feel. For your own personal expression, say exactly what you feel in words you're comfortable voicing.

Get Close and Personal

Ahhhh! Here's where you have an advantage over the greeting card industry. Their objective is to create a card with universal appeal and at the same time compose a message that makes you feel you wrote it yourself. The industry terms this "me-to-you" magic.

Think about your relationship. You're an *original* pair. No couple on earth is exactly like you. What is unique about the two of you? Lovers often devise their own little codes, glances, and goofy pet names. *Pet* names? Classified ads on February 14th reveal some interesting details about relationships. On a single page, valentines were penned to lovers bearing the endearing names of "Snookums," "Punkie," "Puddin," "Hunny Bunny," and "Shuga Booga."

Utilize your own private dialect to sprinkle some intimate me-to-you magic in all your love expressions.

Be Yourself

Be open. Be honest. Be creative.

More greeting cards now feature prose that conveys a feeling of frank, forthright integrity with which the sender identifies. This quality gives the card "pickupability." Although you may still find verses dripping with sentiment, *sincerity* is what editors look for first.

Focus on Your Subject

Avoid comparing your subject with others. Who cares about "all those others"? Certainly not your lover! Tell your partner in simple, sincere, warm words what he means to you.

> Sprinkle some intimate
> me-to-you magic in all your
> love expressions.

What single word appears most often in greeting cards? *You!* Now there's a key word! Make "all the others" a faded memory next to the brilliance of your lover. Fashion the object of your affections as the sole centerpiece for your message!

Make It Your Very Best!

Ask yourself, *Is she worth the effort?* Since 1944, Hallmark has worn their familiar slogan, challenging caring customers everywhere to "send the very best." And it has worked beautifully for them—suggesting quality as well as responsibility. Independent market analysis indicates that it is the most believable commercial slogan in America!

When you dare to give your very best, those

around you recognize and appreciate your supreme efforts. And sometimes it *is* a dare. Expressing true, heartfelt sentiments can often leave us feeling vulnerable and open to possible rejection. Far too many of us avoid such intimate-but-risky dialogue because we fear negative consequences.

In expressing love, your all-out, dare-all attempt wins you the same credibility of the Hallmark slogan. Doesn't that characterize your love relationship—quality as well as responsibility?

Relationships that endure are those whose partners are totally committed in their efforts, energies, and communication. Secure your bond with loving expressions that prove you "dare enough to say your very best!"

21 New Ways to Say the Same Old Thing

"Can't you see my love for you shines in your eyes, lives in your smile, and is here in my arms?"

"I am happy. I am content. I am loved. Why? I am with you."

"Love is knowing that you see me as I really am and yet you still love me!"

"Sometimes I ask myself, *What's so great about this crazy mixed-up world?* Then I remember you!"

"Home for me is wherever you are. When I look into your eyes, I know I'm home."

"When I say 'best friend,' what I really mean is YOU!"

"Could anything feel better than having you in my arms? Yes! Having you in my heart."

"My first choice of all places in the world is close-as-I-can-be-to-you."

"This coupon is valid for one free kiss and a hug. Must be presented in person."

"God gives us such beautiful, perfect gifts. One of His best gifts to me is you!"

"Roses are red, violets are blue; I'll love you for a hundred years—give or take a year or two!"

"Summer and Winter. Spring and Fall. Sunrise and sunset. You and me. That's what a lifetime is all about!"

"We may not always have everything we want, but we do have the important things. We have each other!"

"Completely. Unashamedly. Thoroughly. Without

apology. Without explanation. Without reservation, I'll always love you."

"It's been another year together. Thank you for the 365 times you've made my day this year!"

"You're the ONE-derful part of me I don't ever want to be without."

"I get so caught up with the pressures of life that sometimes I forget how blessed I am to be sharing it with you!"

"When poets wrote of true love and beauty, I dismissed all my heart's intentions. Then I met you."

Explore and practice new ways of saying "I love you."

"Even though life brings many changes, one thing will never ever change: the way I feel about you. It's a forever feeling!"

"Anyone can say 'I love you.' That's the easy part. Finding the right person to hear it seemed to take forever. That happened when I found you."

"You're the sparkle of my eye, the warmth of my smile, the best of my thoughts, the beat of my heart, and the love of my life!"

Read My Lips!

In her book *The Brothers' System for Liberated Love and Marriage,* Dr. Joyce Brothers offers a classic idea for expressing appreciation. Not all admiration for your partner need be communicated with words. Nonverbal communication can be equally— sometimes more—effective!

Proven to enhance your relationships, Dr. Brothers' suggestion also promises to increase your health, longevity, and earning power!

A group of German psychologists, physicians, and insurance companies collaborated on a joint research project. Their objective: to define specific factors of behavior leading to longevity and success.

One doctor summarized their findings. In order to live longer, happier, healthier, and wealthier, you must perform one simple act: kiss your partner every morning before you leave for work.

Is that *all?* Yes, but consistency is the key. You don't have to feel like kissing—just do it.

German researchers revealed that those who kiss their partners every morning have fewer accidents on their way to work. In addition, good-morning kissers are absent less often due to illness than nonkissers. Even more amazing, kissers earn from 20 to 30 percent more and live approximately five years longer.

We all tend to be preoccupied with our schedules and time constraints. It's easy to start the day with negative feelings and doubts about our own self-worth.

A peck. A smooch. A smack. A kiss is a hearty seal of approval. While we express our love with endearing words, cards, candy, or roses, we *seal* our love with a kiss. It verifies positive feelings about our relationship. One kiss provides the warm human touch that words cannot equal.

Extend your life and your love with generous hugs and kisses.

Kissing is often undervalued in our relationships. We assume our lovers will always be there. We forget the power and appeal of a human touch. Let's change that. Resolve to never meet or part without an affectionate greeting. Make a conscious effort to acknowledge your mate, giving new meaning to the well-worn presidential phrase: "Read my lips!"

How to Keep Him "What-I've-Got-at-Home-Is-So-Much-Better!" Kind of Happy

You're starved for his affection. You long for just one tender, appreciative word from him. Lord knows, you deserve it! You'd like to turn him upside down and jiggle him until the praise falls out.

Before anybody gets hurt, consider another alternative: try praising him first.

Hopefully he'll join your chorus of praise. But even if he doesn't, go solo. Sooner or later, there will be a reaction—and it will be a symphony to your ears!

The best way to get him to express appreciation is for *you* to start it. He has likely experienced verbal admiration from other females in his daily encounters. You must ensure he keeps that *"What-I've-got-at-home-is-so-much-better!"* kind of feeling. To make sure you won't be one half of the next separated couple, practice these pointers for polishing your partnership.

Make a "He-Did-It!" List

If he drops off the clothes at the dry cleaners, shovels the driveway, picks up the kids, makes dinner reservations—write it down. Continue to document everything he does for you for at least a week. You'll be amazed at how much he contributes.

Now you have all the evidence necessary to start praising him! Don't shower it on him all at once—he'll drown from the tidal waves. Like spice, sprinkle it gingerly whenever he's least expecting it. Don't be surprised if the "spice" you've added carries over into other areas of your relationship.

Even if he doesn't do everything you wish he *would* do, focus on the tasks he *did* accomplish rather than harping on the chores left undone. Your chances of winning greater cooperation on future occasions will be enhanced.

Make a Date with Him

Once a month, Valerie foots the bill for a night out with her husband, Karl. Valerie makes it a point to verbalize her applause as the focal point for their celebration date. Recently, she thanked Karl for the way he handled the car repairs. Another time, she expressed her gratitude for Karl's extra help during her mother's illness.

Whatever the reason, she makes it a special night for the two of them to remember. Do you think Karl feels appreciated and nurtured? What a lucky guy!

Aim for One "Target Stroke" a Day

Insight counts here. All of us have talents in which we take special pride. And we are particularly pleased when someone special underlines the fact.

Target the areas where your man is sure of himself. Where does he shine? In his athletic pursuits? In his mechanical skills? In his sense of humor? Zero in on the bull's-eye to give your praise maximum impact.

Commit yourself to at least one praise phrase per day. Before the day ends, check to see if you have met your goal. If not, your "pillow talk" is perfect for offering an intimate expression. Now, try accelerating your praise. Set a new goal of saying *three* positive things to him every day. This exercise will help focus your attention because you have to start identifying the good things.

While you may consider compliments "sweet nothings," marital therapists claim these comments contribute a unique ingredient that keeps relationships romantic and lasting.

"Compliments are the glue that hold a relationship together," says psychologist Doris Wile Helmering. "They're one of the best ways partners take care of each other."

Sing Something Simple and Sincere

Keep your praise simple and to the point. A few well-chosen words are much more effective than a lengthy description that may cause him to wonder what's behind your shower of praise.

He has instinctively clear radar for detecting flattery. There would be less *friction* in our lives if there were less *fiction* in our lives. "Be sure your words have the feel of the real," advises Charles Shedd. "He needs the authentic from you."

We need to reassure our mates that we love them exactly like they are. If your guy is paunchy, don't admire his physique. Select something you *do* appreciate, such as his beautiful brown eyes or his dark, curly hair.

Praise something he can recognize as true. Verify something of which he is already aware. If he strikes out every game, don't try to convince him he's World Series material.

Offer your satisfaction by subtle reassurance. A man whose forehead seems to be spreading northward will be pleased to hear you say you don't think a full head of hair has anything to do with sex appeal. Or, if his eyesight has faded from 20/20, reassure him how distinguished he looks sporting his new specs.

Allow your praise to penetrate deeply. Every man wants to be admired for who he is, not just how he looks. In nonsexual situations, men don't enjoy being viewed as sex objects any more than women do.

It takes effort to offer honest praise when he is upset or disturbed about a problem. The last thing he needs is phony praise. The most valuable thing you can do is help him get in touch with his strengths. Do that by reminding him!

Make Positive Contact Through "New Lenses"

Starting today, heighten your awareness of your mate. Put on your "positive lenses" and resolve to see something new about him you haven't noticed before. Challenge yourself to scrutinize those tiny facets you were never aware of before now. Repeat the exercise daily until it becomes habit.

Some of the best things in our relationships are often disguised or even denounced. Look underground, probe deeper in less conspicuous, less obvious places for golden nuggets and strengths you can identify and verbalize to your partner.

Ask His Advice

Rather than telling Kenny she admired his well-built physique, Shari wisely asked his advice about designing her own workout routine. It was the ideal compliment.

Shari accomplished more than one purpose with her creative request. She admired his physique, she has singled him out from all others and she gets the benefit of his expertise.

Flattered by her request, Kenny can offer his advice without any to-do about acknowledging the compliment. Furthermore, Kenny is likely to feel Shari's a discerning, smart lady.

Write Him a Surprise Note

Guys are often so preoccupied with their work or other interests that they forget to really tune in to what's happening now. Arrest his attention by writing a surprise note on a document that's sure to capture his attention—and heart. Send him looking for love in the most unusual and unconventional places.

Ask yourself, *What would my life be like without him?*

If he is a computer buff, leave him a message on his PC or typed on computer paper and inserted between his most important computer printouts.

Imagine him finding a love note in his coat pocket in the middle of a hectic day. Can you visualize him getting an urgent overnight express delivery and discovering your sentiments inside?

If he's a sports fan, make headlines! Pen your message on the sports page. Or attach it to his golf bag, gym bag or the TV remote control.

If he's a businessman, write your message on the financial page alongside the stock exchange data or on the front page of the *Wall Street Journal*. How's that for creating a little news of your own? Then there's always his shirt pocket or his sandwich wrapper.

Turn his "griefcase" into a grin by packing your sentiments inside his attaché. Try penning your praise on the back side of his business card, saying "Lots of love from the other side of you!"

And don't forget the fax of life! Here's where old-fashioned romance and modern technology meet for some really creative options! Fax your feelings to his office—with discretion, of course.

Be Spontaneous!

How quickly we let our partners know when we're irritated. Work at being just as responsive when he delights you. Resolve to always speak in a friendly tone. If your words are soft and sweet, they won't be nearly as difficult to swallow if you have to eat them later.

In his book *Letters to Karen*, Charles Shedd advises his daughter on relationships: "You can only tell him he isn't wonderful where he isn't if you *have* told him he *is* wonderful where he is."

Express how you feel at that moment—even though you may feel differently tomorrow or even an hour from now. Act on your positive feelings spontaneously to create a lot of special moments between you.

Ask Yourself the Ultimate Question

Think for a minute. What would your world be like *without* him? What would you miss *most?*

Jeneanne Sims can answer that question. Before leaving for work on September 5, 1991, Jim shared his good-byes with Jeneanne about 10:00 P.M. outside their Houston home. Stepping back into the house, Jeneanne heard three shots that sent her running outside. Collapsing to the ground beside her wounded husband, Jeneanne held Jim until he died minutes later. Says Jeneanne:

> What do I miss most? A thousand things! After thirty-one years together, I miss his warmth and gentleness and the place I had in his arms . . . I miss holding hands with him in worship services . . . I miss hearing him say 'My pretty precious one, I love you!' . . . I miss being able to tell him anything, everything, things significant and things of no importance . . . I miss the pager he gave me so he could say 'I love you' while I was busy at work . . . I miss his playfulness, his willingness to entertain a whim and go for a hamburger at three o'clock in the morning . . . I miss sitting for hours in the middle of the bed talking, laughing, playing, sharing . . . I miss preparing his favorite meal . . . I miss his slightly off-key rendition of "Jeanie with the Light Brown Hair."

"God gave us memories," says James Barrie, "so we might have roses in December." Jeneanne is enjoying hers now—reliving the fragrance of her years with Jim.

Can you identify with any of Jeneanne's favorite memories? If so, you have more than enough reasons to pay him a heartfelt compliment!

"Share with your love the joy you find in him," advises Jeneanne. "Lavish him with praise and gratitude when he does something for you—even if it's nothing special. Believe me, it *is* special!"

Many women are blessed with an instinct for saying the right things to bolster and assure the feelings of others. They often look at life through their *hearts*. Activate and verbalize your sensitivity to make your man unmistakably sure of his place in your heart!

Give the gift that will outlive you. The special memories you create and the moments you celebrate today may stir the fragrance you'll enjoy for a lifetime.

Remember, you're planting roses. Make them beauties!

How to Keep Her "I-Wouldn't-Trade-Him-for-the-Million-Dollar-Insurance-Policy!" Kind of Happy

It's a dog-eat-dog world out there. Love or money has been the motive for many mystery murders—and not all of them are fiction! With life insurance payouts awarding survivors in multimillion dollar benefits, the unthinkable has crossed your mind. As primary wage earner, could you be worth more dead than alive?

God knows, you're not. But don't wait around trying to find out for sure! Before anyone gets hurt, invest in another brand of insurance coverage—a "home improvement" policy that will guarantee your place lovingly in her heart forever!

Follow these directions for investing and underwriting your own policy—before your beneficiary gets any bright ideas of her own. Make sure she keeps that "*I-wouldn't-trade-him-for-the-million-dollar-insurance-policy!*" kind of affection. As a result, you'll both earn rich dividends.

Just Say *Something!*

"What do you mean, do I love you?" we tongue-tied men have been known to ask. "I married you, didn't I?"

"She knows I love her," Troy rationalizes, "because I don't run around on her or go drinking with the guys," as if that qualifies him for sainthood right behind Mother Teresa.

When a lady looks good and knows she looks good,

she feels good, too. And when a lady is dressed to the nines and her husband *tells* her she looks good, she feels fabulous—which rates better than good!

Problem is, few of us men ever come across with such comments when we should! Why is it many men never fail to notice other women yet ignore their own partners year after year?

When a girl finds a mate, she often exchanges the attention of many men for the inattention of one. Why is it so difficult for a man to express admiration to his wife? Ideally, both partners should give as much praise as they receive, but that kind of equality results from much conscious practice and effort.

Dottie Walters, coauthor of the bestseller *Speak and Grow Rich*, shared with me her own personal philosophy of praise. And it makes for great counsel from a grand lady who ought to know.

"Praise has always worked!" Dottie insists. "My favorite Bible verse is from the last chapter of Proverbs," she relates. "It was written by a woman who advises her son what to look for when selecting a mate. The description matches today's modern woman! The ideal wife is characterized here as having the ability to 'organize and manage her staff, rise early, take care of business, buy real estate, do charity work and take care of her family.' At the end of the chapter, her husband is given one sole instruction that is most often neglected: *'Praise her!'*"

So guys, there you have it—straight from the Book. However inept you may feel singing her praises, she will gladly welcome your expressions of love. And she'll be grateful you cared enough to try. No need to shuffle your feet; just *say something!*

Go Public with Your Praise

Dear Abby once featured a letter from a receptionist protesting that a coworker frequently received flowers at the office from her spouse for no special occasion. A love note was always attached. The writer was annoyed (and perhaps a mite jealous) that anyone would publicly show his feelings this way.

Abby's response is good advice for all men involved in love relationships: "It's a wise and thoughtful husband who lets others know that he loves and appreciates his wife. When a man publicly compliments his wife, the compliment is enhanced."

In his autobiography *An American Life,* Ronald Reagan penned his dedication across the first page in his own handwriting: "To Nancy. She will always be my First Lady. I cannot imagine life without her."

Even Democrats can admire a gentleman who lauds his lady in lovely glowing terms!

One unique trait characterizes enduring relationships: the willingness of each partner to publicly praise the other. If either one occasionally offers a public approval for the other, nothing can shake that union! Look for expressions that speak unmistakably to your lady: *I love you—and you can quote me anywhere on that!*

Write Her a Love Note

Did the last note you left on the refrigerator read: "I love you, darling!" or "We're out of corn flakes"?

Remember, we're grown-ups now. Passing love notes to your best girl is no longer against the rules. In fact, it's encouraged!

The value of documented praise has already been discussed. Nothing you say will mean more to her than discovering your love note on her vanity mirror, on the car seat, in her purse, or on the windshield. "Jim and I were diligent writers of love letters," recalls Jeneanne, a recent widow. "Every day we would leave a message where we knew the other would find it. I have boxes of them and thank God for them!"

The echo of your words has vanished within seconds, while your written praise will be relished over and over.

Write on!

Romance Her with Roses on Tuesday . . .

. . . or Wednesday or Thursday or any other non-occasion, for-no-particular-reason day.

Two male friends, Kirk and Derek, met by surprise in a suburban flower shop.

"So what are *you* in for?" asked Kirk sheepishly, as if they were cellmates just thrown into the slammer.

Why do we men feel that the only appropriate occasion for sending flowers is on Valentine's Day or our anniversary? Or perhaps whenever we've committed some transgression unpardonable by any other gesture? Here we go again trying to buy our way out of hot water—trouble we could have avoided had we acquired the flower habit first.

Flowers have a way with words. But your attention doesn't *have* to be in the form of flowers. Any tangible gift that delights her will be just as effective—stuffed animals, jewelry, collectibles, a figurine, a funny card, a favorite book. Now that you've got an idea, surprise her tomorrow. No, make that *tonight*.

For no reason? Not really. You'll think of something!

Seize the Moment!

After an exhausting day installing a telephone system in a nearby suburb, Neil returned home. Wordlessly, he greeted his wife, Lisa, with an unusually affectionate hug.

"What's that for?" Lisa inquired. Neil shrugged, flashed his infectious grin and explained, "All day I've been working in a house that's a real mess, an absolute tornado. You keep ours so clean in spite of the kids. I just wanted to say thanks."

"I felt like I had earned a gold medal!" exclaimed Lisa later. "You just kill yourself trying to keep up with all the laundry, cooking and housekeeping. And you get the feeling that no one cares. But Neil showed me differently. He really does appreciate what I do."

It's not possible here to suggest a script for your applause. Allow the moment to dictate your word choice. Be sincere; the poetry lies in *how* you say it. Watch the romance bloom in her response!

Say "She's Worth It!" by Your Actions

Actions speak louder than . . . you know the rest. The same thing is true of praise. Sometimes it's easier done than said. One of the nicest things you can do for her is make her life a little easier. Cook dinner, do the grocery shopping, or dress the kids for school. Whatever you do proves that you care enough to provide a little extra space for her. Such unexpected gestures have special meaning and come as a pleasant surprise. Make your praise an *action*—not just a statement.

Take an Active Interest in Her Pursuits

True, you're not really that crazy about needlepoint, opera, or African violets. However, if she has a passion for a particular subject, activity or goal, you'll be miles ahead by supporting her pursuits. Be on the lookout for things she enjoys.

Your daily experiences, periodicals you read and the people you meet may provide excellent sources for adding bits of quality and interest to her pursuits. Surprise her with your thoughtfulness!

Take your interest one step further. Investigate and identify her special interest and plan an event focused around it—a garden show, tickets to the ballet, a weekend flea market shopping spree. Carefully arrange every detail yourself. Attempt to personalize your plans to show extra effort on your part.

Appreciate Your Differences

Vice president of a large bank, Mark provided a generous living for his wife, Sandy. After twenty years of marriage and two children, Sandy decided she wanted a job.

Whatever for? Mark asked himself. *I make a good living. We don't need the extra income.*

Even though there was no financial need, Mark

wisely empathized. He realized Sandy wanted a new challenge—a chance to prove her self-worth to those outside her family circle. Although Mark preferred otherwise, he wisely and lovingly encouraged Sandy in her job search and praised her accomplishments.

One of the greatest challenges of relationships involves the differences between men and women. We don't think alike. We don't respond alike. We don't perceive life's experiences from the same viewpoint. Yet, that is what keeps life interesting—and often frustrating.

Katharine Hepburn once mused, "Sometimes I wonder if men and women really suit each other. Perhaps they should live next door and just visit now and then."

Give her a daily "heart-piece"
to make your love a
lifelong masterpiece.

Understanding differences is often the most difficult kind of appreciation to offer—and the most gratifying for the recipient. It also helps the giver grow.

No couple since Adam and Eve has been the perfect fit. Differences in style or temperament are often what first attracts two people to each other. View the differences as unique qualities in your partner. Recognize the fact that she is a separate personality unit with a unique set of needs, emotions, and behaviors.

Make It a "Heart-Piece"

Evelyn, a widow, recalls that of all the nice things her husband told her, the one she treasures most is, "You're my best friend. I love being with you."

Let her know you appreciate and enjoy the sheer pleasure of her company. It's the supreme compliment!

"Don't tell a woman she's pretty," advises Jules Renard. "Tell her there's no other woman like her, and all roads will open to you!"

"But I'm no good at saying these kinds of things," men often protest. "I just can't say it in words. She knows how I really feel. That'll have to be good enough."

Change that. Your determination and practice will make a difference to her. No one is saying your comments must be literary masterpieces. Just make it a "heart-piece."

Ask the Ultimate Question

Like many other pilots' spouses, JoAnne Speicher was fearful her husband might perish in the fiery skies over the Persian Gulf. Unfortunately, her fears were realized when the admiral and the chaplain knocked on her door bearing tragic news. Scott Speicher was the first American casualty of Operation Desert Storm.

In an interview with Kathryn Casey, *Ladies' Home Journal* editor, Mrs. Speicher revealed the tender emotions of her personal misfortune. In the weeks following the tragedy, a brown envelope arrived containing Speicher's personal effects. Along with his wallet, wedding ring and aviator's wings was a letter dated January 16, 1991—the day before Scott died.

Speicher wrote portions for each of his two young children. Then, he concluded with love lines for Jo-Anne. She'll remember them forever:

"You are the centerpiece of my life. I have lived with you in complete satisfaction. If I am gone, learn to love again."

Think for a minute about your lady and the relationship you enjoy. What would your life be like if she were gone? What would you miss *most?*

Think again. What would *her* life be like if *you* were gone? What words and memories would you want her to cherish most from your years together?

Whatever your answer, have the courage to share it with her. It could be the ultimate compliment of her lifetime—the one she'll never forget. Don't allow your silent, unexpressed appreciation to become the nicest thing that *never* happened to her!

Maybe we make our relationships too complex. Actually, it's the sharing and caring between two souls in search of purpose and fulfillment. And those demands are not unreasonable—just to have trust in someone, to be needed by someone, and to hear an occasional word of love and assurance from that same someone.

No, it's not much. But for JoAnn Speicher—and other ladies—it means everything!

The Book Starts Here

You've read down to the final chapter. Here, the book *really* begins—where your focus comes out of the ink and paper and back to the real world where you live!

Many books promise to do amazing things *for* you. Allow this one to do something *to* you.

Stop reading for a moment. Look around you. What can you do right now—in this precise moment—to breathe new life into your relationships? What steps can we take to generate the positive power that comes in praising people?

You *must* do something now! For those of us who have learned our lessons the hard way, John Greenleaf Whittier acutely describes the bitter pain of omission:

> *For of all sad words of tongue or pen,*
> *The saddest are these: "It might have been!"*

Regrets are the harshest of all punishments. Those we *love* most are those with whom we risk *losing* most. Although we often mask it, each of us craves spoken assurances of love and approval. Like a letter written but never sent, love locked in our hearts can't reach those we love. If we are to succeed in our relationships, they must hear our golden assurances over and over.

Well? When do we start? Unless we use the ideas we've read, then this is just one more book for our library collection. Sure, there's a lot to absorb. Start somewhere. Start anywhere. Just start *now* in pursuit of a higher standard of loving!

Recalling one fall day in 1983, on a Houston airport runway, I've had years to rehearse what "might have been." If, by magic, I could rewind the reel and recall the years, the frame would reveal a far different picture depicting a much wiser man who had read this book . . . and mastered these words—by heart:

"I love you. I need you. You are important to me . . . how else will you know unless I tell you?"

AFTERWORD

From the Desk Of

JERRY D. TWENTIER

There's nothing more rewarding than doing something to enrich and enhance the lives of others! But you like to know when you've hit the target. If reading, applying or sharing this book has been beneficial, I would like to hear from you.

I've become an avid collector of praise stories, miracles and anecdotes—picked fresh from the fields of life. I'm eager to hear *yours!*

How else will I know unless you tell me?

Live with applause!

Jerry

P.O. Box 752524
Houston, Texas 77275–2524

ABOUT THE AUTHOR

JERRY D. TWENTIER has twenty years experience in public, private and corporate training environments. Writer, consultant, professional public speaker and successful business owner, he holds a degree in education from Texas Tech University. Author of more than forty titles, Twentier lives in Houston. He is currently active in human relations/self-improvement training for major corporations.